THIS BOOK WILL TEACH YOU

MARKETING
FUNDAMENTALS

THE INSIDER'S GUIDE
TO MARKETING AND
ADVERTISING STRATEGIES

WHALEN
BOOK·WORKS

"MARKETING IS REALLY JUST ABOUT SHARING YOUR PASSION."

—*MICHAEL HYATT*

CONTENTS

INTRODUCTION. 6

CHAPTER 1:
MARKETING BASICS 9

Five Basic
Marketing Concepts 11

Six Types of Marketing
You Should Know in
Today's Business World. 13

Marketing versus
Advertising. 15

How Will People Find
Out about You? 16

What Is Your Marketing
Message? Six Steps to
Help You Clarify It 18

Doing the Groundwork:
Market Research 20

Six Ways to Help Determine
Your Target Audience 22

Creating a Realistic Marketing
and Advertising Budget 24

Nine Steps for Developing
a Solid Marketing Plan 26

Ten Questions When
Establishing Your Brand
and Brand Story. 28

Setting Regular Times
to Market 31

Ten Great Ways to Start
Finding Leads. 33

CHAPTER 2:
NETWORKING 35

Networking Is about
What You Can Give, Not
What You Can Get. 37

How to Introduce Yourself
without Selling Something 39

Making the Most of
Business Cards. 43

Networking Using
Your Business Connections. 45

Networking Using
Your Personal Connections. 48

The Importance of Word of
Mouth in the Digital Age 50

Five Steps for Following Up
from an In-Person Meeting. 52

Referrals: Giving and Receiving. . . 54

Social Proof and Testimonials. . . 56

CHAPTER 3:
MARKETING AND
ADVERTISING USING
TRADITIONAL MEDIA
AND IN-PERSON
GATHERINGS (YES,
THESE STILL WORK!) . . . 59

Radio. 60

Television 62

Newspapers 64

Magazines 66

The Phone Book
(Seriously?!) 68

Business Sponsorships 70

Helping Charities
and Nonprofits. 73

Direct Mail Campaigns 75

Press Releases 77

Flyers and Brochures. 79

Public Ads and Billboards. 81

CHAPTER 4:
MARKETING AND
ADVERTISING USING
SOCIAL MEDIA AND
THE INTERNET. 83

Types of Internet Marketing 84

Using Your Website to Best
Advantage 89

SEO versus SEM:
What's the Difference? 92

Social Media Dos and Don'ts . . . 97

CHAPTER 5:
MAKING THE
MOST OF EVENTS 102

Events of All Kinds:
Ten Ways to Be Prepared!. 104

You're Not There to Market!. . . 107

Why Non-Networking Events
May Be Better for You. 109

Professional Conferences 112

Trade Shows 115

Round Table Events. 118

Entrepreneurial Events 121

Industry-Specific Talks
and Meetups 122

Get Involved with
Community Service
Group Events 124

Casual Get-Togethers 126

Charity Events and
Fundraisers. 128

RESOURCES. 130

Further Reading. 131

Online Resources. 133

About the Author. 137

INDEX 138

ABOUT THE
PUBLISHER 144

INTRODUCTION

This Book Will Teach You Marketing gives you the basics of the often confusing and conflicting world of marketing. Marketing is absolutely necessary, but it can seem absolutely terrifying at the same time! With endless potential customers to reach, and seemingly endless ways to try to do it, how do you choose the right ones? Help! This brief guide will offer you advice and instructions for getting started and show you how to reach out to those potential customers and clients that will be most receptive to your unique message. Remember that marketing is above all about cultivating good relationships; it's not about what you can get, it's about what you can give.

We'll look at one of the most important subjects any business faces today: making enough professional noise to attract attention, clients, and customers. The world of marketing seems to get more congested with each year. The time-honored media of television, radio, and magazines are still going strong; advertising remains a multibillion dollar industry in North America and beyond. Add in the jumble of social media sites and platforms, blogs, podcasts, videos, and everything else you can think of, and the possibilities to market seem endless. Yes, that can be overwhelming, but it's also encouraging. There have never been more opportunities to make your voice heard, but you have to do it the right way, and that's where this handy guide comes in.

The information here is ideal for small businesses and smaller companies that don't have a marketing department. Whether you're marketing for a company or your own business, you'll learn the basics for finding your "people," targeting your campaigns for the right groups, creating solid marketing plans, making a memorable impact on your desired audience, and allowing yourself to stand out in a crowd of competitors, where everyone is screeching to have their messages heard first. You don't need to be the loudest or get your message out to everyone in the world; you just need to have a good plan and strategies tailored to your own needs. Some of this advice you may know and some may seem obvious, but it's important to remind yourself that marketing is an ongoing process, not a one-time job on the destination to success. Marketing efforts can easily go wrong and end up wasting time and money, so let this book help you market smarter; with some work, you might be amazed at the results!

The book is divided into chapters grouped by subject. Each offers important information and gives you a starting point. Consider this book as a quick-reference and handy guide when you want to look up something about a specific topic. Feel free to dip in wherever you like, and read the book in any order that helps you. Of course, this survey can only offer brief summaries, but you can use the information here as a good jumping-off place for further research and education. Keep in mind that this book is not a substitute for legal or other official advice, and if you need further help on any of the topics here, you will need to seek it out on your own. The Resources section at the end provides a lot of helpful further reading, as well as useful websites that can give you far more information than a small book can. This book is your doorway to a much bigger marketing world!

Marketing sometimes seems confusing and baffling, and you may be tempted to throw in the towel and ignore it. Don't! The basics here should help ease some of your fears and ensure that you're able to make a splash about your business, while cultivating great new relationships and experiences along the way.

> **"Do what you do so well that they will want to see it again and bring their friends."**
>
> **—WALT DISNEY**

[CHAPTER 1:]

MARKETING BASICS

What is marketing? What isn't it? These questions
have simple answers, but like any subject, the more
you dig into it, the more you know that you don't know.
And if you don't know anything, don't worry; you've
come to the right place! This book introduces
you to key concepts and ideas, as well
as offering practical advice to get started.

So again, what is marketing? The American Marketing Association (AMA) defines marketing as the "activity, set of institutions, and processes for creating, communicating, delivering, and exchanging offerings that have value for customers, clients, partners, and society at large." The goal of marketing is to establish a brand and a reputation for the product or service you're selling, and use that to increase your profile and sales. The way that's done is by creating relationships that will improve connection and move businesses forward.

At its heart, marketing focuses on providing people with both needs and wants.

NEEDS

Needs are what people require for daily life, as well as feelings of stability and safety. They include actual items, such as food, water, and shelter, or they can be psychological needs, such as love, acceptance, family support, friendship, and self-esteem.

WANTS

Wants are the things that people desire for themselves but are not necessary to survive. A large part of marketing is focused on wants, since much of what we buy and consume is not based on basic survival requirements (no, you don't *need* that expensive pair of shoes, no matter how much you think you do!). Wants are often influenced by factors such as our surroundings, what our peers have, and others' opinions. They're not always rational, that's for sure!

DEMANDS

A demand for something is created when a need or a want is supported by the ability to obtain it. If a group of people want a particular new car and have the ability to pay, then there is a demand for this year's model.

This chapter explains some of the key marketing concepts to give you a good introduction to just what you'll be doing as you start to wave your hands around and shout: "Here we are!" Whether you want to do that literally or not will be up to your overall marketing strategy!

FIVE BASIC MARKETING CONCEPTS

> Marketing concepts come and go, and there seem to be an endless number of them, but these five tend to hold their place and importance over a changing background.

1. **Production Concept.** This concept relates to production of goods and focuses on the idea that a business can lower its costs by mass production. Producing a large amount of a thing that consumers want results in a lower cost for that thing and lowers costs for the company. A bottle of a popular soda is a good example. It's also something that almost everyone is aware of.

2. **Product Concept.** This concept involves the idea that when customers want something of a certain quality, they will be less concerned about its price and availability. The latest cell phone or laptop are good examples of this in action.

3. **Selling Concept.** This concept focuses on selling (obviously!), specifically on selling as many as possible, regardless of the product's quality, or the customers' actual wants and needs. Think of how much cheap junk you see for sale all the time! Someone is making money from it, or they wouldn't keep producing it.

4. **Marketing Concept.** This concept specifically addresses the wants and needs of the customers, and puts them first. By doing this from the development of the product all the way through to the sale, the company is able to deliver exactly what its customers want and need, which inspires loyalty and repeat business.

5. Societal Marketing Concept. This newer concept focuses on the idea that the well-being of customers, and of society, is important in the product being marketed. This concern for the whole can affect things such as budgets, profit margins, and company image, among many other considerations. Marketing something as "good for the environment" is a great example, as is donating a portion of profits to a charity. Younger consumers are often attracted by these promises, but they expect the company to actually deliver on them!

> **"Ignoring online marketing is like opening a business but not telling anyone."**
>
> **—KB MARKETING AGENCY**

SIX TYPES OF MARKETING YOU SHOULD KNOW IN TODAY'S BUSINESS WORLD

There seem to be so many marketing types and categories that the mind boggles. These six types are by no means the only kinds of marketing out there (some websites list dozens of other kinds!), but these are increasingly important in the changing world of marketing and are forms you should be familiar with as you move forward in your marketing education.

1. **Influencer Marketing.** Influencer marketing, as the title suggests, involves the use of individuals who have some form of influence over a potential target group of buyers, and using that influence to deliver the brand's message. An example would be a sports star endorsing a line of sports shoes or active wear. This individual (actor, athlete, musician, other celebrity) becomes the face of the product, and it sells by association.

2. **Relationship Marketing.** Again, as the name suggests, relationship marketing is about building relationships with specific groups of customers, building loyalty to a brand and keeping them for the long term. This can be done in a lot of different ways: discounts, gift cards, frequent buyer or flyer programs, loyalty programs, implementing customer feedback, and many more.

3. **Green Marketing.** Green marketing delivers an environmental message that will appeal to certain group of customers. Terms like "non-GMO," "organic," "recycled," and so on are used by companies that follow these practices and want to connect with and attract customers who share their values.

4. **Keyword Marketing.** Keyword marketing is the placing of a message in front of users based on keywords and phrases they are using in their online searches. This can be ads (such as banners) related to something they're searching for or search engine optimization (SEO) so that one's website comes up at the top of a search. In both cases, a keyword is used to direct someone to a site, and deliver a message to a potential customer.

5. **Viral Marketing.** Viral marketing is so named because it spreads, kind of like a virus, from person to person. It's a form of word-of-mouth advertising (in person or through social media) that takes advantage of social proof—the more that people talk about a product and praise it, the more others see it as having value. A company can encourage its customers to spread the word about a new item and let those customers do some of the marketing work for them.

6. **Guerilla Marketing.** Guerilla marketing relies on low-cost and often unusual tactics to deliver a message. Viral marketing is often seen as a form of guerilla marketing, but there are other kinds, including stealth marketing (advertising something without the person realizing they're being marketed to, such as product placement in movies), grassroots marketing (starting with a small group and letting them spread your message), and ambient marketing (placing ads or products in places you wouldn't expect to see them), among others.

MARKETING VERSUS ADVERTISING

So, what's the difference between marketing and advertising?

Marketing is the background work, the research, and the analysis of how to make sure a proposed product aligns with the wants and needs of a target audience. It's the process of preparing the product or service for a marketplace, and bringing together all of these elements in an attempt to identify potential buyers with the product or service a company is offering. When you do this, buyers are happy with what they receive, and the company makes a profit. Everybody wins!

Advertising, on the other hand, is really a component of marketing, and a very important one. It's the part of marketing that actually gets the word out about your product, the one that shouts, "Hey, over here!" and tries to attract those potential customers that you've targeted. If you've done your marketing research properly, your ads will be focused in specific media and will reach the people you want to reach.

> **"Good marketers see consumers as complete human beings with all the dimensions real people have."**
>
> **—JONAH SACHS**

HOW WILL PEOPLE FIND OUT ABOUT YOU?

So, you have a product or a service that's excellent, and you want others to know about it? Of course you do! Before you can begin working on marketing your awesomeness, it's good to understand a bit about how people find out about things they're interested in. Here are a few of the most common ways they do so online.

- **Internet Searches:** Someone wants a specific item, and you have it. Not only that, you have the best version of it! So, by using keywords and SEO, you position your website to come up at the top of an internet search. This is great because you already have someone interested in the product or service, and if you're coming up at the top of the heap, they're probably going to check out what you have to offer.

- **Good Reviews:** A great form of free advertising. If someone is looking for something on Yelp or Amazon, or anywhere that allows customer reviews, and they see that you're getting large amounts of five-star ratings, it's going to make you look very good. The downside, of course, is the danger of disgruntled reviewers or trolls trying to sabotage your success, but if you're delivering quality, that's not too likely. You'll never please all the people all the time, so living with the occasional negative review just comes with the territory. Unless the reviewer has a legitimate complaint, try not to take them personally.

- **Browsing:** Reaching out to people who are browsing online can be an effective marketing tool, if you do it right. Getting your message or ad onto a site, article, video, or similar bit of media that is related to what you are selling can interest users who might have come just for the content. In the real world, this might involve going into a store and seeing a product you didn't know you needed. The idea is to position yourself in areas where your product is related to what the browser might be looking for.

- **Your Advertising:** Everyone seems to hate ads, but they're still effective. Advertising is a multibillion dollar industry, so clearly at least some businesses are doing things right! Yet forcing your product into a YouTube video or a spam email can be risky. If you start getting a reputation as spammer, you'll not likely get rid of it, so don't spam, ever! Advertising works, but you have to be smart about it. We'll discuss ads later in the book.

> **"Many companies have forgotten they sell to actual people. Humans care about the entire experience, not just the marketing or sales or service. To really win in the modern age, you must solve for humans."**
>
> **—DHARMESH SHAH (COFOUNDER, HUBSPOT)**

WHAT IS YOUR MARKETING MESSAGE? SIX STEPS TO HELP YOU CLARIFY IT

Before you can market anything, you have to decide on what it is that you're trying to communicate. This should seem obvious, but doing it is a bit trickier than it seems. Here are some ways to help you define the story you want to tell, so that when you're ready to go after customers, you have the best and most persuasive message you can offer them.

1. **Decide on your target audience.** If you don't know who that is, you're not going to get very far! What is your product or service? Who will it benefit? Who wants it? Who needs it? Why should they care? Contrary to what you might think, just saying "everyone wants this" and leaving it at that will do you no good. The more well defined your potential audience and customer base is, the better.

2. **What is the main value of what you offer?** Your focus needs to be on the benefits you provide, not the features that you think make your product cool and amazing. Those are all well and good, but people want to know what's in it for them. If they buy your product or service, how are they benefiting? That's the key point to keep in mind: benefits, not features. No one cares much if your software has an intricate and crazy design; they want to know how it's going to help them.

3. **Who's competing with you?** Who else is offering what you offer, or at least something similar? And don't say "no one," because there will always be something out there that resembles your great idea. That's not a bad thing; you'll always have competition. So, what is their message? What kind of quality are they bringing to their products? How could you do it differently, or better?

4. **Create a message/statement (probably several of them).** Keep it clear, concise, easy to remember, timely, and geared toward your target audience. Sure, no problem! Remember, you're not trying to offer your product to the entire country (nice as that would be!), you're trying to hone in on those who most want and need what you have to offer. Give them something short and sweet, and they'll thank you for it. You may have more than one message, so prioritize them, according to what you think is most important. This whole process is going to take a while, so don't rush it. You may leave it for a bit and come back to find that you'd rather emphasize something else. That's OK!

5. **Test out your message(s).** Give them a go in the real world, see who responds and why. Try working with small target groups and volunteers. See what clicks and what doesn't. A lot of producers of movies and even TV shows offer test screenings to gauge an audience's reactions, and then they go back and fine-tune. This is a good model, so use it.

6. **Refine them again.** Keep tweaking your message until you're getting the results you want and it represents what you offer. Then, it will be ready to roll out!

DOING THE GROUNDWORK: MARKET RESEARCH

Remember having to do research papers in school? Or bigger projects in college? Yeah, if you're involved in marketing, you'll never really get away from that. Doing the necessary background research is essential to defining your product and who will be interested in it. To do this work, you'll be engaging in primary and secondary market research.

SECONDARY RESEARCH

Secondary research is often the best place to start. It really is just analyzing data that's already out there, stuff that you don't have to do any work for, because the work's already been done. This data can be anything from published studies in journals or on websites, to opinions on social media. Basically, if it's written down somewhere, you might be able to use it. It's a good way to find out who your competition is, how well they're doing, and what you could do to be better. Is there even a want or a need for what you'd to offer? If not, then you may need to rethink your plans and go back to the drawing board. If you can establish that there is a market, you can move on to primary research.

PRIMARY RESEARCH

Primary research is, as it sounds, your best and most useful form of research. It can involve a number of strategies, some of which we'll look at here:

Surveys and questionnaires

Companies offer surveys all the time, on websites, on paper, even at the end of phone calls. They're a useful way of getting instant feedback that can then be tallied and analyzed. They tend to work better with larger groups. A survey of twenty-five people won't tell you as much as one with five hundred people, for example. Questionnaires tend to be a bit more detailed but also yield good results.

Interviews

Interviews can be very revealing and allow a company to determine exactly what a customer wants, from the horse's mouth. They are conducted either in person or over the phone, and can be great for getting deeper into a subject, especially when you want to find out what someone *doesn't* want.

Focus groups

Think of a focus group as group interviews. A selection of people in the target market are brought together in a room or other space, and a moderator leads the discussion (more recently, online focus groups have become a thing). The people are usually compensated for their time, and can offer invaluable information about a product or service. Again, this is a great chance to find out what people don't want and how a product or service can be improved.

Field trials

When you're much closer to a launch, this kind of research can be helpful. A simple example would be an A/B trial. You put out two different versions of the same ad to a control group and find out which one resonates with people more. Field trials can, of course, be way more complex than that, even involving scientific studies, but if you're a small business, you probably won't need those just yet.

SIX WAYS TO HELP DETERMINE YOUR TARGET AUDIENCE

As mentioned above, you can't just assume that everyone will be interested in what you have to offer and leave it at that. No matter how much we'd like to believe this, the fact is that there are always going to be people who just don't care about what we're selling; yes, it seems ridiculous, but it's true! Having a well-defined, even narrow, target audience and list of potential customers will be much better for you in the long run. Here are some ways to narrow down your focus and find the right people for you.

1. **Compile data and information on your current customers.** If you have current customers, this is a great place to start. Using the primary market research tools mentioned above (pages 20–21), try to get a sense of what's working and why. Who are they? What do they want? What don't they want? Are they part of a specific target group (age, location, economic status, etc.)? What are they already buying from you that they could use more of?

2. **Consider the product or service you are offering to help you identify a target.** Whether or not you have existing customers, consider your target's demographics: What is your product, and who is it going to serve? Who needs what you have to offer? Who will be most interested, and who will least likely be interested? Eliminating unlikely target markets can save you a lot of time and money going forward. The goal is to narrow it down, even into niche and specialty markets (each of which might require different marketing strategies).

Just make sure that the niche is not so small that it's not viable; forty-five people may be a unique and specialist market, but it's probably not going to be a profitable one!

3. Consider your potential customers' psychographics.

Psychographics differ from demographics in that they take into account qualities that are harder to define with data: personality, interests, habits, opinions, lifestyles, and so on. These are important considerations, because you want to understand *why* your customers want what they want, not just that they do. Psychographic data can be obtained during the market research phase, especially during interviews, focus groups, and questionnaires (see page 21).

4. If you have social media accounts, use those sites' analytics to determine who is interacting with your accounts.

Pretty much every social media site has some form of data analysis built into it, and you can use this to help narrow a potential target market further. If they like your page or follow you, they're already interested!

5. Whom are your competitors serving?

Who are their customers, and how is your potential group of customers both similar and different? Can you use those differences to your advantage? Is there something you are offering that they are not? You don't want to go after the exact same group, so what can you do to diversity it?

6. Evaluate and refine.

Even after you've found your target market(s), you'll probably decide that it can use some fine-tuning. It's always good to revisit and see if your previous choices are still relevant, or if you need to change as the audience does. The hottest thing now may not be so much next year, and you need to adapt. It's an ongoing process that isn't just finished one time.

CREATING A REALISTIC MARKETING AND ADVERTISING BUDGET

The budget for your marketing will largely depend on the size of your business. But even a for a large company, the marketing department will probably want to be careful and conservative at first in working out the total costs. Here are some ideas for keeping things on track while also getting the most out of the budget you do have.

- **Be very sure about your budget.** What are your incomings and outgoings? How much do you clear per month? Does that amount vary a lot in different months? Are their times of the year when you're better off (there usually are)? What is the smallest amount you make in any given month, after your other expenses have all been met? This is sometimes known as "reliable revenue," and is the baseline for your budget. A percentage of this number is what you have to work with, and if you have a better month, welcome it as a bonus! There may be certain times of the year when you are doing well, but these may not the best times to start a big marketing campaign (though online activities such as blogs and social media should be done all throughout the year). Conversely, the ideal time for your marketing could happen when you're struggling. Consider these potential problems and use your money accordingly. Set aside some funds if you can.

- **Be very sure about allocating your funds correctly.**
  Where do you want to spend your money? This will require
  extensive research and probably some trial and error to determine
  which marketing strategies work best for you. If you have a small
  budget, stick with small expenses. Don't blow the whole thing on a
  glossy magazine ad or some other big expense. Spread it around
  to many less ambitious areas: online ads, paid social media and
  blog posts, a newspaper listing, press releases, etc. You'll likely want to
  spend a significant portion on internet options, since that's where so much
  of everything happens these days. If you're still testing the waters, you'll
  have to spend money on some strategies that don't work as well until you
  find the best fit for you. It's just part of the cost of doing business, but in the
  end, you'll have fine-tuned your marketing strategy better.

- **Accept that you'll probably have to spend a bit more at
  the outset and budget accordingly.** As outlined above, you'll
  need to test the waters a bit if you're a newer business, but this testing
  should always be line with your overall goals and your market research.
  Don't try out random, crazy marketing ideas just for the hell of it! There's a
  place for being unconventional and experimental, but in the early days, it's
  best to stick with tried-and-true methods. Once you've accumulate enough
  data for a marketing campaign, have seen what worked and what didn't,
  and developed a better sense about the habits of your target markets, you
  can branch out and tailor new strategies to specific groups or needs for
  your next marketing efforts. And maybe try something crazy.

- **Compare your efforts with those of your competitors.**
  This falls under the research portion of your budget, but it's an important
  point to remember. What is your competition doing? Is that working for
  them? If so, can you emulate their methods? If not, how can you improve
  on what they're doing? Having successful competition is a good thing
  in this case, since you have existing models to see what works and what
  doesn't. There's almost always room for improvement, and you should
  always be on the lookout for a way to do things better.

NINE STEPS FOR DEVELOPING A SOLID MARKETING PLAN

Now that you've collected some key information and identified some of your own goals, it's time to think about developing a good marketing plan. Having a well-thought-out plan is essential going forward. You'll want to bring together what you know so far. A good marketing plan should include the following information, which will be far more detailed in your plan than it is here.

1. **Define your business goals.** What are you hoping to achieve through marketing, and how will this help you achieve those goals? Define your goals and a realistic timeline for achieving them. This might be ninety days, or six months, or a year—whatever you feel is best and most doable. Make sure you can track your progress on these goals, and mark important successes along the way.

2. **Write a good business summary.** Who are you? What do you do? What do you offer? This summary should also include what's known as a SWOT analysis, detailing the Strengths, Weaknesses, Opportunities, and Threats that pertain to your business. What's great about what you do? What needs improvement? What's your potential for growth? Is a competitor already doing things better than you?

3. **Identify your target markets.** You've probably already done a lot of this work, so put that information here! You may be going after more than one market and will need to tailor your marketing to the needs of those different groups.

4. **Identify strategies to reach that market.** What will you do to get your message to them? How will you promote yourself? What media will be the most effective in reaching them? This is crucial, because you can waste money on ineffective methods and squander your budget and chances early on.

5. **Who are your competitors?** Identify who is offering a similar service or product. What do you offer that they don't? Can you improve on what they offer?

6. **What is your budget?** How much can you spend on marketing? Are there things that can be done inexpensively, or even for free (yes, a lot of them!)? Do you have a maximum limit? If not, you should (see pages 24–25 for more information on budgets).

7. **Make sure everyone is on the same page.** Do you have colleagues or supervisors? Do you have investors? Anyone else who has a stake in the business should know what the plan is; you may have to be accountable to some of them. Keeping everyone in the loop is a great way to prevent uncomfortable problems later on.

8. **Understand builder and driver campaigns.** Builder campaigns recur and are geared toward the longer term. Things like blogs, social media posts, and newsletters remind people of your existence and that you're doing cool things! Driver campaigns are more immediate, lasting a month or two, and are designed to meet specific goals. These can be about an event, a product launch, and other time-sensitive happenings.

9. **Develop an execution plan.** Identify the tasks that need to be done in order for your plan to be implemented, and make a commitment to doing them! Create a calendar and stick to it.

TEN QUESTIONS WHEN ESTABLISHING YOUR BRAND AND BRAND STORY

Your brand is basically how others see your business. It's not just your company logo or a cool, recognizable name. It's your reputation, which will appear right away. It's something you'll build over time as you interact with customers and clients. You'll use various marketing strategies to build your brand, such as your website and SEO, social media, and email. We'll discuss these in more detail throughout the book.

When defining your brand and your story, ask yourself these important questions:

1. **What is your purpose?** Why are you here, and what are you going to offer? You have to have an identity, and if you don't know what you're doing and what your goals are, why should anyone else care? What motivates you? Do you have a mission statement? If not, draw up one! Be prepared to tell your story; describe what got you started and what you're passionate about, and share some of the good and the bad times. Humanizing your brand allows others to relate to it.

2. **What solutions are you offering?** If there's a need or a want, what are you doing to meet that? Are you offering something new or a cool spin on an old solution?

3. **How are you different?** What are you doing differently from your competitors? How can you do it better? Research their products and services thoroughly to see how you can stand out. List some specific benefits that your business brings that are unique to you or that are offered in a unique way.

4. **Whom will you target?** What groups have the needs and wants that you wish to fulfill? Try to make these demographics narrow and well-defined. Just saying "students" or "programmers" is far too wide, and won't allow you to zoom in on niche markets that you could really serve well. Who is your ideal audience? Who is your dream client? Focus on making these concepts really clear. Your audience will grow over time, but start out on the smaller side and get into the details.

5. **Why should people care about what you do?** What makes you stand out? What makes you better than another company? You have to toot your own horn and show what it is about your business that makes it special.

6. **Do you have a unique voice?** What's the nature of your brand? Professional? Highly technical? Causal? For the young? The older? Understanding these qualities about what you offer will help you craft your own voice tailored to your customers and clients.

7. **Do you really understand what it is you're offering?** Do you have a thorough understanding and knowledge of your product or service? You'll run into trouble if you don't. This requires getting into details, even if there are similarities to other products on the market. The sellers of a BMV understand the differences their cars have from an economy-style car that sells for less than half the price, for example: a different kind of vehicle, a different customer base, a different car culture, etc. Ignore this information at your own risk.

8. **Are you being consistent?** In developing your story, you need to be consistent not only in your behavior but also in your identity. Do you have a logo that you use everywhere? A tag line for all of your communication? Consistent posting and online presence across social media platforms, with a recognizable presentation in all of them? These are all very good ways to be consistent. Make the effort and spend the money to craft a good overall look for your business, including a nice logo and an attractive design that are consistent on your website and social media. These elements send a very good message that you're serious and have your act together. Just as important is developing a good reputation for your practices, ethics, and attitudes. Treat people well, offer a quality product, do it with sincerity, and they will remember. That remembrance will become associated as with your brand as you grow over time.

9. **Are you constantly refining?** By necessity, your brand strategies will change over time. Are you keeping current and analyzing your progress? Are you trying new things to see what works? Are you abandoning old things that don't? Being able to adapt is crucial to your survival and growth.

10. **Is co-branding for you?** When you're starting out, it might be worth your time to partner with another business or organization to deliver a common message. The idea is that you can reach a larger group of people and help each other grow. Nonprofits are often good to approach with this strategy. If you have shared values and can offer their audience something they can't, it may be beneficial to you both.

> # "The best marketing doesn't feel like marketing."
>
> *—TOM FISHBURNE (FOUNDER AND CEO, MARKETOONIST)*

SETTING REGULAR TIMES TO MARKET

Marketing and all of the factors that go into it can seem like a bit of slog when you first approach them. But in today's competitive and fast-paced business environment, leaving things too long will leave you behind. Small businesses and entrepreneurs often spend a whole day each week devoted to marketing. Companies that rely on repeat and new sales may spend 50 percent or more of their time on it since it's so critical to their success. So what can you do to make sure that you stay current, keep yourself in the spotlight, and don't miss good opportunities? Here are a few ideas.

- **Do marketing work every week, or, even better, every day.** How much you do and what you do will be largely up to your budget, your goals, your products, and your available time, but it's important not to skip marketing tasks or avoid them for too long. If your business needs new customers and increasing sales, you'll especially want to be mindful of this. Some of it may be fairly simple work, such as posting to your social media pages, writing a short blog, or looking at the analytics for those sites. This seems small, but it adds up over time. Your tasks may be more complex, such as working on target demographics, conducting surveys, and so on. But even a little every day is better than nothing. The goal, of course, is to be doing more than a little every day!

- **Try keeping tasks to a regular, weekly schedule.** Post a new blog every Wednesday (or whatever day works best for you). Post new social media content on Mondays, Wednesdays, and Fridays, if those seem like good times. Set aside a day for networking. Set aside a weekly time for research into current trends. None of these have to take a particularly long time, but keeping them regular makes them into routines, and with enough repetition you won't even think about it; it will just be a part of the day's tasks.

- **Prioritize tasks and set deadlines.** What needs to be done first in your weekly marketing work? Get it done first. Create deadlines for specific goals and keep them. If you know you have to finish certain tasks by certain dates, you're more likely to keep to that schedule, rather than just having vaguely defined goals. If your goal is to define three new potential target markets by Friday, setting a deadline to get it done will keep you on track.

- **See things through to completion.** It sounds kind of simple, but creating checklists will help you to keep ahead of tasks. Ticking off things as you finish them brings a sense of satisfaction and allows you to keep track of your progress. And it gives you bragging rights when you've ticked off all the boxes!

- **Investigate what's not working and correct it.** Have you been trying a particular strategy and finding that it's not getting you the results you want or any results at all? It may be time to rethink it or even drop it altogether if it's not serving you anymore. This is fine. Sometimes strategies work in one case, but not in another. Don't be afraid to move beyond a particular strategy, even if it's a well-proven one for getting results. It may not be a good fit for what you're trying to do.

TEN GREAT WAYS TO START FINDING LEADS

The ways of generating leads are essentially endless, but some methods work better than others. In this day and age of the internet being ruler of all things, lead generation can be even easier. Here are some of the most commonly used methods to go about it.

1. **Email:** Mailing lists are still a great tool for getting your message out. Allowing visitors to sign up for your list in exchange for something of value (a download, a link; see page 90) is a time-tested and proven way to grow your list.

2. **SEO:** Optimize your website with keywords to ensure that it shows up at the top in internet searches (see page 86).

3. **Social Media:** You'll want and need a presence across multiple social media platforms: Facebook, Twitter, LinkedIn, and maybe YouTube and Instagram. The details will be up to you, but you need to be there.

4. **Blogging:** Having a regular blog (attached to your website) where you post news and helpful information will keep customers and potential customers coming back (see pages 85–86).

5. **Networking One-on-One:** Meetups for coffee, lunch, happy hours, days out, sporting events, and similar engagements can be ideal for generating possible leads (see pages 126–27).

6. **Networking at Events:** Conferences, trade shows, and talks all provide excellent opportunities to meet new people in your industry (see pages 112–23). Whether you meet colleagues or competitors, prospects or mentors, use these kinds of events to really get to know new people and get yourself and your business known.

7. **Marketing Automation Software:** There are many programs and tools that can help make your marketing efforts easier. Take the time to familiarize yourself with some of them and see how they can help.

8. **Exclusive Website Content and Calls to Action:** These little bonuses are great for getting new people to sign up for your mailing list or to interact with you on social media. Create a poll, offer a small prize in exchange for an email address, and get your followers involved!

9. **Case Studies and Success Stories:** List these on your website, blog, newsletters, and social media pages to demonstrate the value that you offer in the real world. It's all well and good to talk about how great you are, but people need to see proof. Did your product or service directly benefit a client or customer? Are they willing to talk about it? Get that information and get it out there!

10. **Word of Mouth:** Nothing beats having someone say something nice about you, whether in the real world or online! Creating a business worthy of this kind of unsolicited praise is the challenge, and should always be one of your goals (see pages 50–51).

[CHAPTER 2:]
NETWORKING

Networking is the name of the game. Marketing
without networking probably won't work or at the very
least it will be a lot more difficult. Beyond just marketing,
networking pays off in many other ways: it opens you up to
meeting new people, sharing ideas, and possible collaboration
or integration into other projects later on. It may expose you
to some heavy hitters who really can bring new opportunities to
you in the long run. It will make you a better professional, as you
may need to improve your own skills to keep up with your peers
and competitors! It will also make you better in your own life, as
you'll likely become a better people person. If you're an introvert
or uncomfortable around crowds, there are ways to network that

don't call for immersing yourself in a sea of people. Indeed, some of the best networking you can do is one-on-one chats over coffee or lunch. Within the vast realm of networking, you'll be able to find a style that suits you. And you'll realize that it all gets easier the more you do it.

There's no one right way to network, though there are definitely many wrong ways! As you'll see in this chapter, one of the first ideas you have to get rid of is that networking is about you and getting what you want. Of course, if you open up new doors, you will potentially bring new opportunities to yourself eventually, but what if you go into each new encounter with the idea that you want to bring your value? What if you go into each new meeting with the idea that you can offer your help and your expertise? What if you meet someone, see their problem, and come up with a solution? By being a giver rather than a taker, you not only bring some good into the world, but also you build trust and the potential for long-lasting relationships. And that's the ultimate goal of any networking that you do.

So, let's delve into networking in more detail!

> **"Networking is not about just connecting people. It's about connecting people with people, people with ideas, and people with opportunities."**
>
> **—MICHELE JENNAE**

NETWORKING IS ABOUT WHAT YOU CAN GIVE, NOT WHAT YOU CAN GET

It may seem counterintuitive at first, but networking really is about what you can do for other people. Whenever you meet a potential new contact, client, partner, friend, or customer, your first thought should never be: "What can I get from this person?" Rather, be thinking about what you can offer them and what you can do to help them. Creating genuine relationships built on trust and mutual respect will gain you far more in the long run than making fancy pitches in pursuit of a quick contact or sale. Here are some ways to interact with new people that let you offer up yourself as a genuine source of help and benefits.

- **Make the effort to reach out.** This seems obvious, but many people never even begin the process, due to fear, indecision, distractions, procrastination, and a lot of other manufactured reasons. By taking the time to locate and contact people that you want to establish communications with, you're already showing that you value them. Be sure to explain why you're reaching out to them and how you found out about them. Knowing that you've singled them out for attention is a great little ego boost, and fosters a feeling of trust and friendship from the start.

- **Listen to them.** Your contact may have a fascinating story to tell; listen to it. It may be relevant to you or it may not, but studies have shown that genuine listening develops empathy. And you never know, they may be able to offer you help on a problem you've been dealing with, even without intending to do it. The more you listen, the more you learn.

- **Offer advice.** You may want advice from them (and may even get it), but also be prepared to give it. You might just have the perfect solution to a problem they've been struggling with, and that builds a strong connection right from the start. They may have questions for you; do your best to answer them. You may have specialist knowledge that they may not have access to, and if you can share it (legally and ethically, of course!), that builds a great relationship.

- **Offer outside connections.** Networking is about making connections, but it's also about the potential for sharing mutual connections that may offer each other benefit. If they have a problem or a task, and you know someone who could assist in just that area, offer to connect them. They'll likely do the same for you. Maybe there's an upcoming event that they would be interested in attending but don't know about; be sure let them know. Is there some tool (such as an app or software) that might be useful to them? Show it to them!

- **Value them.** This should go without saying, but contacts are valuable and should always be treated that way. You're not in the business of using people to get what you want (and if you are, that needs to change); you're in the business of making meaningful connections that will help others, and eventually come back to help you and your company. Word of mouth is still a powerful thing. If you foster a reputation for being helpful and sharing, it will get around. If you're seen as selfish and self-serving, that will also get around, and it's a lot harder to come back from that!

HOW TO INTRODUCE YOURSELF WITHOUT SELLING SOMETHING

What can you do when making a new connection to keep from turning it into a sales call or email, or an in-person pitch? How do you present yourself as genuine, as someone that this potential contact not only wants but also needs to know? Here's what to do to be sure you don't come across as a used-car salesman.

- **Email:** Email is a primary means of business communication. Reaching out to people via email feels a little safer than having to phone them, but the downside is that it's one step removed from the personal touch. Emails can get caught in spam filters, be ignored, or be filed in the "get back to it later" category (and forgotten about). What can you do to make sure that your email stands out?

  - **Write a good subject line.** It's what they'll see first, so make it quick and attention-getting. Avoid anything to do with networking or selling, and instead offer a benefit: "Lunch on Friday?"; "Love your work, do you have a few minutes?"; "Reaching out about the XXXX project."

- **Tailor your greeting to the specific person.** This is absolutely crucial! An email beginning "Dear Sir" or "To whom it may concern" will 99 percent of the time end up in the trash. Find their name and use it, and for goodness' sake, spell it correctly!

- **Make your intro about them first, you second.** Mention something they're doing (and even your admiration for it), then introduce yourself.

- **Explain why you're reaching out.** But again, make it more about them than you, and if possible, offer to help on something.

- **Use your call to action.** This could be "Can we meet when you have time?" or even a request for a follow-up email conversation to keep things going. Whatever seems best.

- **Thank them for their time and sign off.** That's all you need. Keep it simple.

- **If they don't respond, it's OK to follow up.** Some say to wait three days; some say to wait a week. Go with what feels best and send a polite follow-up, maybe offering a bit of help. If they respond, great, but your follow-up may still not get you anything back. That may not be a problem; some studies have shown that it can take three to five requests to get an answer! It really depends on how important this potential contact is to you and how much you want to keep reaching out to them. You don't want to become a nuisance, of course, so proceed carefully!

- **Phone:** Phoning people can be uncomfortable or even downright terrifying for many. What if they don't like you? What if they laugh at you? What if they yell at you and hang up? To be honest, these things are pretty unlikely ever to happen. Happily, the format for these isn't all that different from an email.

- **Greet them, introduce yourself, and ask if this is a good time to talk.** It might be, or it might not. If not, ask when a good time to call would be, and if you can schedule a quick phone chat. You may be asked how you got their number, which could come across as a bit blunt, but if the person in question is getting dozens of calls a day, they probably don't want their number shared widely. A simple, honest answer is the best.

- **Acknowledge that you're reaching out to them, and are interested in starting a conversation.** No pitching anything!

- **If it seems appropriate, briefly outline what you or your company does, and how it benefits others, particularly how it might benefit them.** Just a very quick outline, no extensive details; you don't want to bore them!

- **If the conversation continues:** Great! You're on your way to developing a new relationship. The person on the phone may be your best contact, or they may offer to put you in touch with someone better suited. In that case, you have a referral, so be sure to mention it to the other person.

- **If they're not interested:** Thank them for their time, hang up, and move on.

- **In person:** In-person meetings are obviously the best way to connect with someone, but they can be fraught with problems if you feel awkward, lack confidence, aren't comfortable with face-to-face contact, or any number of obstacles. These meetings often come about as a result of an email or phone conversation, so the initial introduction part of it is already out of the way. That's good news! They're meeting with you because they want to discuss things with you further. If you schedule this kind of meeting, it might be nice to keep it informal: lunch, coffee, etc. An initial meeting is unlikely to be a formal affair, but be sure to dress well and be on your best behavior. You're building a friendship, not making the hard sell. Refer to "Networking Is about What You Can Give, Not What You Can Get" (page 37) for some guidelines on how to conduct yourself in this kind of meetup. It's all about listening and forging a genuine connection.

> **"Our job is to connect to people, to interact with them in a way that leaves them better than we found them, more able to get where they'd like to go."**
>
> **—SETH GODIN**

MAKING THE MOST OF BUSINESS CARDS

Business cards are still a thing, even in our heavily digitized modern world. The idea of a small but tangible object is still appealing to most of us. In some countries, such as Japan and China, business cards are essential, and the proper design and presentation of them to new contacts is crucial to getting a new relationship off on the right track. If you mess it up, it can seriously damage your future chances of working together. Can a good business card or other media help you in the networking game? Yes, it absolutely can! Everyone uses their phone these days, but having a card, a physical object to give out, makes the meeting much more personal. Here is some helpful advice on business card etiquette.

- **Always have business cards with you.** You never know whom you'll meet and what circumstances might come up. Be prepared and expect the unexpected!

- **Have a professional design.** It doesn't have to be super fancy or expensive, but don't just design them yourself (unless you have those skills) and print them out on tear-off sheets. Make the (small) investment to have professional cards printed up and make sure they are the standard size. Unless you have a very quirky or unusual business, the simple, rectangular card is your best choice. You want to make a good impression.

- **Include necessary information, but not too much.** Your name, your company, your phone number, and your email address are all essential. Beyond that, a website and/or Linked In profile might be useful, or you can have those embedded in a Quick Response (QR) code, which lets the recipient of your card scan it with their phone and be taken to the link right away. A tag line about what you do can be good to include, but keep it short and to the point. You don't want a cluttered card! Allow for sufficient blank space around the writing.

- **Choose whom you hand them out to carefully.** Have them on hand, but don't just give them to everyone. Have a strategy, and make sure that your cards only go to people with whom you want to connect and with whom you've already broken the ice and shared a little rapport. Just tossing them at people will do you no good if a significant connection isn't established first.

- **Always ask for their card in exchange.** The idea is to open up a potential new relationship, and that only works if you both have each other's contact information. If they don't have one or don't have any with them at the moment, get them to write down their contact information for you, which means you should also have a pen and something to write on handy, even if it's the back of one of your own cards.

- **Consider giving them two cards.** This way, they have one to pass on to another of their colleagues. This is especially good advice if you've had a conversation and things are going well. Your new contact may have a boss or team leader that might want to know more about you, and they can pass on your information while keeping a card for themselves.

- **Have some friends, colleagues, and family members help you out.** Give out a small number of cards to people in your personal circle, because you never know when they might meet someone who could use your services or be a valuable contact! The people closest to you are often your biggest cheerleaders and can't wait to tell others about what you do!

NETWORKING USING YOUR BUSINESS CONNECTIONS

Without a doubt, much of your networking will be done through your business and business contacts. That's where you will meet many like-minded people whom you can help and who in turn may open doors for you. Here are some ideas for taking advantage of an existing business structure to help you when networking.

- **Know the different kinds of business networks.** There are several different kinds of networks in a business environment, including:

  - **Casual networks:** These are groups and organizations that offer general get-togethers, often with a theme but not specific goals. Chambers of commerce are an example. These gatherings can be great places to meet informally, with little pressure and no need to consciously network.

  - **Contact networks:** These are smaller, more focused groups that usually include one specialist from each industry that they want to include. If they do have meetings, these will be more useful for networking and the exchange of cards and information. An example would be, say, a real-estate broker whose contacts include a gardener, a general contractor, an appraiser, a lawyer, and a roofing service— basically one business of everything involved in the sale and maintenance of homes. If you

can become a part of one of these networks, there's no competition, and your business will be the go-to contact when anyone asks for a referral. Hooray! Of course, to get into one of these exclusive clubs, you'll have to provide something of great value, since others' reputations will be on the line if they recommend you.

- **Professional associations:** Professional associations are most often devoted to a single industry or area, and may not permit outsiders. Some, however, do allow associate members, but remember that your goal is to form connections, not make sales pitches!

- **Social media:** This includes LinkedIn, Twitter, and Facebook—anywhere that you might meet potential customers or new colleagues.

- **Make yourself contactable.** Your business email should have a signature with all the ways to contact you. You want to be found easily and also have the information readily available if someone wants to view your LinkedIn profile, your work profile, and so on.

- **Have a good message on your phone's answering service.** This may seem odd, but think about it: if someone new is calling you and goes to voice mail, this will be the first time they hear your voice. Listen to your existing message and be honest with yourself: Would *you* want to talk with you? Keep it brief, but keep the tone inviting and friendly. You want to appear welcoming. Speak clearly and make sure your voice is understandable.

- **Keep your online bios updated.** You want to include your latest accomplishments and achievements. Keep your photo updated as well; don't just use that good one from four years ago! Strive always to make a good impression if and when people seek you out.

- **Write for your company newsletter or blog.** If you have good ideas and feel comfortable writing about them, get them out there and be seen. Establishing yourself as a subject matter expert is a great way to give yourself credibility and makes reaching out to others that much easier.

- **Attend other business networking events.** There may be other gatherings in your area besides the ones listed above. These can be great places to meet up with others who are also there looking to make contacts. Have your business cards ready, and be prepared to mingle and start conversations. Be sure that you know what your own goals and aims are, and be ready to listen to others and offer help if you can.

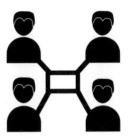

> **"You can have everything in life you want if you will just help enough other people get what they want."**
>
> **—ZIG ZIGLAR**

NETWORKING USING YOUR PERSONAL CONNECTIONS

It's also possible that your network of friends and family may be of use in reaching out and forming new connections. After all, this group of people can already vouch for you (we hope!), and knows more about you and the work you're doing than just about anyone. Here are some suggestions for people you can reach out to in your own life, outside of your company or business.

- **Family:** An obvious first choice, but who knows you better or wants you to succeed more? Siblings, parents, cousins, and others may be great sources of leads. Do your parents have loads of contacts they've made over the years? They probably do! Do you have a sibling working for a cool new start-up? Ask about their needs. Referrals from family can be an excellent way to open new doors!

- **Friends:** If you're fortunate enough to have a good circle of friends, consider what they do for their work and see if there might be any good fits for your own goals and what you or your business are offering. Maybe you have a friend already in marketing, or someone with experience in sales and advertising. You never know who is out there until you ask!

- **College and university contacts:** Don't leave out people from your college days. Did you have a particular teacher that you admired? Try reaching out and telling them what you're doing now; it may open doors. Do you have university friends with whom you've lost contact, or just don't see as often as you'd like? Try rekindling those friendships and see where it takes you. You may be able to offer something to them in exchange.

- **Former coworkers:** If you've had one or more previous jobs, there may be coworkers with whom you're still friends or at least on good terms with. Offer to take one to lunch and catch up on old times. See what they're doing now and if you could fit into it in some way. Did you and your old boss get along well? Hit them up and offer to reconnect.

- **Volunteer and community organizations:**
Do you volunteer or work with a charity of some kind? This can be an excellent opportunity to meet like-minded individuals whose goals and values align with your own. Just be sure you're not signing up to work at one of these organizations with the sole purpose of trying to worm your way in and make sales or gain advantages. You're there to help that organization meet its goals, but in doing so, you might find that there are ways in which you fit in. Your work, product, or service may be of value, if not to the charity, then to others in it. Build strong relationships first, and then let things happen, if they do.

- **Social media:** If you have a page or site with followers, try reaching out to them in a general notice (but be careful about spamming!). It doesn't hurt to get the word out about what you're up to, and you might be surprised at who's already following you.

THE IMPORTANCE OF WORD OF MOUTH IN THE DIGITAL AGE

Whether we call it word of mouth or something going viral, in-person recommendations and endorsements are a great way to expand your reach. Many would say that technically marketing and word of mouth are two different things, and this is true. Marketing is more about the work that you do, while word of mouth is about letting something take its course after the work is done; it's letting your network market for you, which is a beautiful thing, if you've set it up correctly!

Endorsements of this kind can be very beneficial. It's estimated that, even in our highly online-oriented world, there are more than three *billion* mentions of brands every day in North America (Canada and the United States) alone. That's an astonishing number and shows that personal recommendations still carry a lot of weight in promoting a company's message. If your best friend buys something and loves it, you're probably more likely to try it yourself than just seeing a random ad for it somewhere. The human touch never goes out of style.

Word of mouth can grow organically, but it's also helped along by your reputation, and that's something over which you have a lot of control. It goes back to the way you approach your business and your goals. If the goal is only to get something for yourself with little regard for those around you, your reputation is going to suffer eventually. Sure, some people build businesses this way, but you want to be able to sleep at night and live with yourself!

But, as we've seen here, if you approach networking as a way to give—to pay something forward—that's going to make a lasting impression, and it's going to be remembered. There's a saying to the effect that people may forget your words, but they will remember how you made them feel. Strive always to make new contacts and potential customers feel great, feel valued, and feel important, and you'll make yourself memorable.

"You will get more word of mouth from making people happy than anything else you could possibly do."

—ANDY SERNOVITZ

FIVE STEPS FOR FOLLOWING UP FROM AN IN-PERSON MEETING

If you've been fortunate enough to have an in-person meeting with a potential client, partner, customer, or anyone else, and it all went well (we hope!), what's the next step? It's crucial to follow up shortly after that meeting to keep the conversation going, and it's good to have a set way of doing it. Here are some useful steps to take.

1. **Send a personal email within twenty-four to forty-eight hours.** Twenty-four hours is probably better. Keep it brief, and thank them for their time. Mention a part that was a highlight of the conversation for you, especially if you laughed and joked about something, or found common ground. Right after the meeting takes place, it's useful to jot down a few notes or impressions you had that you can refer to later in your email. Just make sure that your message is professional and edited properly; you don't want to send something with typos and other mistakes. Second impressions count, too!

2. **Offer your help.** If they've mentioned a problem or issue they're having and you happen to come up with a solution later, definitely mention it in your follow-up:

   > "Hi Joan, It was great to meet you yesterday; how crazy that we went to the same high school! I've been thinking about your issue with XXXX, and I think this might work . . ."

   Making this kind of offer instantly creates rapport and shows your value and willingness to reach out and offer assistance. It's the kind of thing that won't be forgotten. But even if you don't have anything like the answer to their prayers, even offering to be around to bounce ideas off of in the future is a great way to let them know you are there for them.

3. Send a handwritten note. Doing this on some nice stationery will make quite the impression! Hardly anyone sends actual letters anymore, so taking the time to thank them and let them know they are valuable by using this kind of physical outreach will definitely stand

out. Just think about how impressed you would be if someone did this for you! Be sure that your handwriting is legible and you don't come across in any way that would make the person feel uncomfortable. It's also good to send a follow-up email, too. Avoid sending anything like a gift or other token, since this could be taken the wrong way.

4. Offer to connect online. Extend the offer to connect on LinkedIn. Your personal social media pages should be left out of it, but if you have a company Facebook or Twitter page, you could suggest they follow it, in exchange for you following theirs.

5. Offer to stay in touch and meet again, if they're amenable. If the meeting went very well, it's probable that they'll want to meet up again, especially if you've found common ground. If it seems like the right thing to do, suggest another meeting at the time and place of their convenience. If this isn't practical or possible, make the effort to stay in touch anyway, even if it's only once every thirty days. A monthly or quarterly check-in helps prevent you from drifting apart and losing touch, and you never know when you might get the recipient at exactly the right time. Make your follow-ups more meaningful by sending them something relevant to them, maybe an article or a blog that you think they'd be interested in. Have you met someone recently who you think would be good for your contact to meet as well? Offer to introduce them.

REFERRALS: GIVING AND RECEIVING

Referrals are a wonderful way to meet new people, open doors, connect with potential clients and customers, and be noticed. As with so much in business and life in general, you get back what you give out. Referrals are a form of word of mouth, whether general or quite specific. There's nothing better than when you hear that your hard work and attention to other's needs results in them recommending you to their friends, colleagues, business partners, and others who could help your business. But you can't just sit back and wait for them.

- **Referrals often require more than just your casual attention.** If you have a colleague who is in need of something, and you think you know someone who might have a solution, you'll need to understand their problem well enough to be able to confidently make that referral. Also, you need to understand the solution the other person or business is offering. You don't want to waste either party's time. It could be something as simple as recommending your accountant to a friend who needs one, but it could be as complex as a large business needing some kind of new software program. Make sure you know what both parties need and are offering.

- **Offer referrals to companies and businesses that you're happy with.** This seems obvious, but the more you can recommend others and their services, they more they will flourish, which is just what you want for yourself. If they are colleagues of yours, it's great to let them know that you're sending potential new business their way; they'll probably be delighted! But make sure you're not doing it in a way that says you're expecting them to return the favor. This shouldn't be a mutual back-scratching exercise, or some insincere and devious way to bring in more clients for yourself! Make a commitment to helping others, and you may find that when the time comes, they're willing to help you, too. And on that note . . .

- **The best referrals are the ones that just come to you.** If you're doing your job well, you'll probably find that others out there are already recommending you, in person, on social media, and elsewhere. This is great, and it's a sign that you're doing the right thing. However . . .

- **It's OK to ask your clients and customers for referrals, but be sure you've earned them!** If you're committed to providing great service and genuine care for others, there is nothing wrong with asking your satisfied customers to recommend your services and potentially send new clients your way. But don't be pushy about it, and take the time to develop good relationships with them first before asking. Also, don't expect them to keep doing it. Once is fine. If they do so again, it means they really like you and trust you, and you have a good relationship. But that's a bonus, not an expectation!

SOCIAL PROOF AND TESTIMONIALS

Social proof is basically the notion that others will change their behaviors and habits according to what they see around them. We see this every day. If a coffee shop has a line out the door, you're likely to be persuaded that their coffee must be very good! If someone on social media raves about a certain thing, it may not be long before lots of others are doing the same, prompting even more people to want to check it out.

As it relates to your business, maybe you've started getting good Yelp reviews, or maybe your social media page has gained a good number of likes and follows in a short time. This is great, and you want it to continue! We all love when others say nice things about us, but we can really take it personally when someone says something negative, even if it's a business or company that's being targeted.

So how do you get those sweet favorable reviews? It's simple: getting good testimonials is all about what you deliver. Give them a quality product or service, and you're likely to hear back about how good it is!

Social proof can come in several forms:

- **Expert endorsements:** Does someone in the know approve of your product? Great! Are they willing to say good things about it? Even better!

- **Celebrity endorsements:** When someone famous gives you the thumbs-up, this can be gold, because it immediately signals to that person's fans that you have something they might want, which saves you the trouble of having to tell them! When their followers and your market overlap, it's a beautiful thing!

- **Public testimonials:** Sites like Yelp, Amazon, and other review sites can be great for letting people sound off on why they think your product is so great. Bring on those five-star reviews! Of course, this always brings the risk of negative and one-star reviews, but that's just the nature of doing business. Not everyone is going to like you, and some trolls will actively seek to trash you for the fun of it. Be great enough so that their ugly voices get drowned out by a wave of goodwill!

- **Good press:** Does local or national media have something to say that paints you in a good light? Fantastic! An interview, a short story or feature, or, if you're lucky, a longer story . . . all of these are fantastic ways to get noticed.

- **The "wisdom of the crowds":** As the name implies, this has to do with following the crowd, though how "wise" they are is up for debate. If a lot of people are excited about something, other people will want to know why, which eventually makes even more people excited about it. This plays into the sense of Fear of Missing Out (FOMO) and encourages people to see what the fuss is all about.

- **Social media:** Another kind of public testimonial. If your page posts are being shared a lot, it means that people are into them and care enough to pass on what you've said. This feeds back into the wisdom of the crowds. Celebrity and expert endorsements can do very well on social media, too. One tweet from a major star praising you or what you're doing, and it may reach hundreds of thousands, if not millions, of people.

When using social proof in your marketing efforts:

- **Avoid negative social proof.** This is when you present a negative message (in and of itself not always a bad thing, but it has to be done right) and back it up with statistics or numbers that suggest that it's fine to do it anyway:

  > "XXXX is a bad thing. Last year alone, more than one million people did it. Don't be like them. Our product will keep you from doing that thing."

  This may seem like a good strategy, but it usually backfires. Don't use this kind of language to suggest that missing out on your product will make them like countless others who also missed out. Let's be honest, a lot more people didn't buy your product than did, and they're all presumably doing fine! After all, if a million people did the bad thing that you don't want them to do, it can't be too bad, can it?

- **Focus on positives in your message.** "We supply XXXX. With more than 10,000 satisfied customers and a 93 percent rate of buying again, we are confident in all of our products. Let us show you how XXXX can work for you!" See how much more effective this is than the negative version? Always focus on positives when relaying information to your market. There's enough negativity in the world as it is, so don't put any more out there!

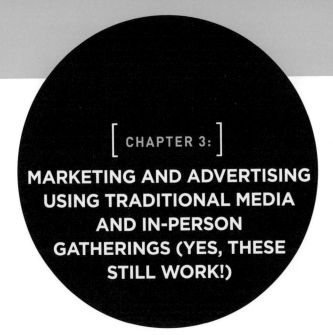

[CHAPTER 3:]

MARKETING AND ADVERTISING USING TRADITIONAL MEDIA AND IN-PERSON GATHERINGS (YES, THESE STILL WORK!)

While everything seems to be going digital these days and the internet rules over all, there can be many advantages to focusing some of your time on the more traditional ways of advertising. Radio, newspapers, magazines, television, and more are still a big part of mainstream society, and it's very likely to your benefit to at least explore using these formats to get your message across. How much time you want to put into each and how much money you have to do so will depend on your own schedule and budget, but a bit of old-fashioned advertising might be just the thing once in a while. Since more and more people seem to be abandoning these methods, it might even help your business to stand out just a bit more!

> While the heyday of radio may be long over, it continues in many forms, from traditional to digital to internet versions. Television didn't kill it, and neither did the internet. It remains a powerful presence in the lives of many, one that you might be able to use to your advantage. There are more than nine hundred radio stations identified across Canada, in English, French, First Nations, and other languages, so there is a potentially big scope for you to reach a large number of people.

It's estimated that at least two-thirds of Canadian listeners work full-time and have the radio on while they do, which gives you a great captive audience to get your message out there. In fact, radio ranks only behind television in Canada as the public's main entertainment experience; up to a third of people's media time is spent listening to radio of some kind. Here are some of the common types of radio stations and broadcasts.

- **Analog:** Traditional radio stations still abound, with CBC being the obvious largest collection of stations. Discussions about making CBC completely advertisement-free are ongoing, with some wanting to phase it out completely in the next several years. Recent reports show that the average adult in Canada listens to up to fourteen hours of traditional radio per week, so there is great potential in this old but trusted medium. Some stations, such as campus radio, limit the amount of time that can be devoted to advertising in a given week (just over 500 minutes at the moment), while other formats, such as community radio, have no limits. If you want to advertise on these platforms, you'll need to contact individual stations and see what is permitted and what the time frames are.

- **SiriusXM Radio Canada:** Sirius Canada is a Canadian affiliate of Sirius XM Radio. SiriusXM Radio Canada offers around 130 channels. SiriusXM serves over sixty-five million listeners, and claims that its ads can be heard in Canada, the United States, and Mexico. However, recent studies have shown that Sirius listeners overwhelmingly prefer ad-free music channels and are less responsive to ad-driven stations. It may still be worth your time to investigate, but do your research before buying time with them.

- **Internet:** Large numbers of traditional stations also offer their programming online through streaming, which is great for increasing their audience size further, even outside of Canada. The number listening to streamed radio services is on the rise, with the average Canadian adult tuning in to seven hours a week or more of such content. When coupled with listening to traditional radio programs, the number of hours per person now reaches as high as twenty-two. Depending on which format they are listening to (ads or commercial free), there is the potential to have your message heard by a growing audience.

Tips:

- **Do your research and see what times of day are most effective for your ad.** Does your target demographic have a favorite show? Consult with the station and see. Are some days of the week better than others? Usually, it's good to pick a certain show or time of day, and run your ad consistently.

- **You're more likely to reach your targeted listeners or get their attention through repeat airings.** This is true even if the ad is short, say, less than thirty seconds.

- **Don't expect immediate results.** You might get some, but researchers advise that it can take a few months to really sink in and make an impact. Radio advertising aims for the long haul, so be sure your budget can accommodate it.

TELEVISION

Television also offers a number of advertising opportunities, though these will cost substantially more than radio ads. Your budget may not extend at all to television, and that's fine. The merits of advertising on TV are always being debated, but for most small businesses, if they do venture into the world of TV, it will be on local channels with a limited reach, which is probably the market you're looking for anyway. There are now nearly eight hundred TV stations across Canada in all formats, and that number will only increase in the coming years.

- **Local:** Realistically, local and regional television stations are going to be your best bets for advertising, if you decide to go the TV route. Many are affiliates of bigger networks (just as in the United States) but also offer local programming, and there are a decent number of independent stations, too. Here, the possibilities are numerous, as you can tailor your message by region, city, language, and so on. Many are available in both analog and digital formats in a variety of languages.

- **National:** Major networks such as CBC, CTV, Global, Ici Radio-Canada Télé, TVA, and Omni Television are all major players on the national TV scene. National advertising is expensive and complex, and if your company is considering going for this kind of advertising (and is at the point where it's worth doing), you'll probably be using the assistance of an advertising agency or some similar company to help you. This is not something you're likely to just have a go at alone!

Tips:

- **As with radio, choose your target audience(s) carefully.** TV advertising can be considerably more expensive than other media, so you won't likely be running ads for the same duration as you might on radio, though most stations will lock you into a contract for a specified period of time.

- **Consider working with the station or network to determine the best times and programs for you.** They'll have information on demographics that can help you.

- **Some local stations will offer to produce the ad for you as a part of the ad price, which can be a great help if you don't have access to a camera and studio of your own.** If you go this route, be

  sure to view some of the other ads the station has made to make sure they're up to your standards of quality. You don't want a shoddy-looking ad going out to represent you. It doesn't matter who produced it; the viewer will associate it with your business.

> **"Nobody counts the number of ads you run; they just remember the impression you make."**
>
> **—BILL BERNBACH**

NEWSPAPERS

While physical newspapers increasingly seem like a thing of the past, they're still popular with many demographics (especially older generations) and shouldn't be ignored as possibilities for marketing and advertising. Fortunately, most Canadian print newspapers also have online versions, which makes using them in your marketing campaigns far easier and more immediate.

Newspapers Canada (see **Resources**, page 135) is a great online resource for learning more about the Canadian newspaper industry.

- **Local:** As of mid-2019, there are more than one thousand community newspapers across Canada, publishing about sixteen million copies (!) of their editions a week. Studies from a few years ago suggest that nearly three-quarters of Canadians who live in nonurban areas read a community paper regularly. The vast majority of these papers are free and rely on advertising to stay alive. Depending on the type of business you have, this could be a potential gold mine for reaching out to smaller communities. The majority of these papers have online versions as well, which makes their reach much larger.

  Another great advantage to local papers is that they always need new stories. Do you have an exciting announcement, product launch, charity event, or other gathering coming up? Reach out to your local paper and see if they'll do a feature about it. It's a great opportunity to get exposure and tell your story in more detail than an ad can give you.

- **National:** National papers such as the *Globe and Mail*, *Toronto Star*, and *Le Journal de Montreal* still have print circulations in the lower hundreds of thousands, while nearly two dozen other papers across the country have circulations from about 30,000 to 180,000. These are good numbers if regional or national advertising in print form is within your budget, though for many of these papers, their circulation numbers are dropping little by little each year as more readers prefer online sources of news. But online versions won't be going away any time soon, and choosing to advertise there may be your best bet, if you're ready for a national audience.

Tips:

- **Make your ad distinctive.** You may not have that much control over where your ad is placed (unless it's for a specific product that is tied to a section of the paper), so you have to make sure that it stands out. This doesn't mean that it should be flashy or busy! Choose the ad size according to your budget (you'll probably have several options). Obviously the bigger you can make it, the more it will stand out, but this may not always be feasible. A good image can sell the whole thing, so work with your designer to figure out what's eye-catching. It's usually best **not** to let the newspaper design the ad for you. Only you know what you want and how you want it to look.

- **List the benefits in your ad.** You're amazing. You know it. But they don't, and they probably don't care yet. Instead, tell them what's in it for them. That's all they need to know.

- **Keep it (relatively) brief.** Depending on the size of the ad, you may not have room for too much text anyway. So inform readers without giving them a dissertation. People give up if they feel overwhelmed.

- **Include a call to action in the ad.** While you need to highlight your product or service, you also need to be inviting so that the viewer *wants* to purchase or at least wants to learn more. This can be anything from "call now" to "visit our website for a free gift." Be creative and think of ways you can lure in new prospects.

MAGAZINES

You might think that magazines, like newspapers, are on the way out. Readership has been declining in recent years, but according to *Magazines Canada* (see **Resources**, page 135), recent studies have shown that the largest consumers of print magazines (in terms of issues read per month) in Canada are in the age range of eighteen to twenty-four. The next two age demographics (twenty-five to thirty-four and thirty-five to forty-nine) are the next highest. About 80 percent of all Canadian magazines published are consumer-oriented, while the remaining 20 percent are business and trade magazines. Trades may be a particularly good option if your business markets to specific industries, rather than to the general public. Most larger-circulation magazines have online versions, too, but these are usually behind paywalls and require subscriptions to access. That's not a bad thing; subscribers have a genuine interest in the subject, and you'll likely find a more receptive audience to your ads and marketing efforts if people are paying for their content.

- **Local and Regional:** There are large numbers of small and specialist magazines, probably something for everyone. These can be ideal resources if you have niche markets—as always, the smaller and more defined, the better. As with local newspapers, magazines always have a need for stories; use this to your advantage if you have exciting news to share. A feature, whether online or in print, will give you great exposure to a target audience, and, best of all, it won't cost you anything!

- **National:** Choosing to advertise in national publications can be a great option if your budget allows for it and your business is at the point where it would be a good return on investment. Again, you'll want to narrow the scope down to those periodicals that are related to your industry in meaningful ways or are devoted to markets where you want to be known. Online ads may be more cost-efficient, in terms of reach, but don't discount print-version ads if you really have something important to say. As with local magazines, scoring a feature or story in a national magazine is a fantastic way to get your message out. Of course, convincing a national magazine with a large circulation that you're worth their time is a bit of trick; you'll also be up against a lot more competition for space, especially in the print version. You'll have to be doing things that are truly newsworthy and appeal to broader sections of the population.

Tips:

- **Follow the same guidelines as for newspapers (pages 64–65).** Most of that advice applies to magazines, too.

- **You might have more control over where your ad is placed in a print edition.** This can be beneficial if you are targeting markets related to specific magazine features. Positioning may also be based on costs; obviously, the back cover will cost much more, since you'll likely be expected to buy the whole page.

- **Consider your design even more carefully.** If the magazine publishes in color, it gives your ad a better chance of standing out, if it's creative, attractive, and designed well. Don't skimp on this! Use a professional to design it.

THE PHONE BOOK (SERIOUSLY?!)

Honestly, are phone books even used by anyone anymore? Surprisingly yes, mainly by older demographics. But let's be honest, the number is shrinking in both Canada and the United States, and if you're looking into advertising in this very old-fashioned way, you'll have to consider your return on investment, which is actually pretty hard to track with directory listings. Unless every single person who buys your product specifically tells you how they found out about it, you'll have no real way of knowing if a phone book listing made any impact at all.

While there are digital (i.e., online) versions of phone directories, the traffic for these sites pales in comparison to that for the major search engines. A majority of people who receive physical phone books admit that they don't even bother to open them, which just seems like a big waste of paper and trees! But old habits die hard, so they keep getting printed, year after year.

Often online phone book contracts lock you into a whole year, and there have been numerous stories in recent years of businesses feeling that they've been scammed by shady phone book offers and contracts. All of this for ads that most people will never even see.

So, the bottom line is, unless your product or service is specifically geared toward an older audience (and there's nothing wrong with that; it's a valuable demographic!), you'll probably want to give the old-fashioned phone book a miss. There are far better and more cost-efficient ways of marketing and advertising that will bring you better results. Back in the day, the phone book was crucial to getting yourself noticed, but not anymore. If you're old enough to remember how thick they used to be versus how thin they've become in the last two decades, it should tell you all you need to know about how many businesses still consider them a valuable advertising tool. Honestly? Not that many.

> **"Telephone books are, like dictionaries, already out of date the moment they are printed."**
>
> **—AMMON SHEA**

BUSINESS SPONSORSHIPS

Business sponsorship is an increasingly effective way to improve your brand recognition and get your message in front of new people. It might be an event, a concert, a conference, or some other form of social engagement; all of these offer opportunities to be noticed, and just as importantly, the chance to give something back to your local community. You might think that to sponsor an event, your company has to be loaded with money. This is not true; most events would be delighted at even a modest offer of help. While you won't likely be hosting a party with major rock bands appearing, sponsorship can take many forms.

You might be one of several businesses offering support, or you may only be responsible for just one aspect of the whole affair. It's important that the event is one that you feel comfortable being associated with. You might choose to sponsor something that everyone can take part in, such as a weekend festival or craft fair. Maybe it's a chance to bring together a bunch of great local bands for a daylong concert that lets them gain new audiences. Just about anything can be an event worthy of your time and attention, if it's something you believe in and especially if it will attract people in your targeted demographics.

And that's an important point: you'll need to pick and choose events that will be attended by those who will be interested in your product. There has to be some overlap, or you're just wasting your time. You'll need to consider age groups, backgrounds, locations, and a dozen other factors to determine just how well the event aligns with your target markets. Likewise, it's crucial not to associate yourself with anything shady or scammy. If you're hearing rumblings about an event being unethical or doing illegal things, steer very clear! You want to be seen in the best light, so only associate yourself with events that have an excellent reputation.

Beyond the importance of getting involved in your community, here are some reasons to lend your support to these kinds of gatherings.

- **It puts you in a good light locally.** If your event is indeed something for a specific location, you have the chance to contribute to the neighborhood, the town, or the city. That makes you a good neighbor and shows that you can be trusted. If you can be trusted, your marketing message will be better received. Once again, you're building relationships.

- **You can advertise your sponsorship across social media and your mailing lists.** An upcoming event gives you a gold mine of opportunities to spread the word on the internet about your involvement. Social media posts and emails can link to event pages or other sponsors (that way, everyone gets noticed). You might even consider partnering up with some of your cosponsors, so that you can each spread the word into new markets and mailing lists that you don't normally have access to.

- **You can advertise your involvement via traditional media.** As outlined in other entries in this section, you have the chance to make use of more traditional forms of marketing to get the word out: press releases, flyers and brochures, radio spots, direct mail, and more.

- **It separates you from your competition.** Do you have a competitor who is not sponsoring an event? So much the better! It might give you the chance to interact with the attendees in a way that the competition can't, especially if you can have a booth or other promotional material at the event.

- **It may allow for networking with complementary businesses.** If your competition is not present but other businesses are offering their own kinds of sponsorship, what can you learn from them? Is it worth making new connections? Might there be chances for future partnerships, collaborations, or sponsorships? Always be open to exciting new encounters!

- **You can offer endless kinds of promotional material, depending on what the event is.** Obviously, this depends entirely on your product and your budget, but the possibilities for free giveaways and gifts are almost limitless: pens, tote bags, coffee mugs, software samples on USB sticks, phone cases, T-shirts, promotional literature, yoga pants, email list sign-ups, contests to win prizes (especially if your product can be one of them!), etc. Whatever you can imagine and afford can be brought to the event, and will make you memorable in the minds of the people attending, way more so than just reading a boring ad online or in a magazine.

> **"Marketers need to build digital relationships and reputation before closing a sale."**
>
> **—CHRIS BROGAN**

HELPING CHARITIES AND NONPROFITS

> As with business sponsorships, giving time to charities and nonprofits is a great way to raise your company's profile and give something back to your local or regional community. Just remember that you are going into this kind of partnership with the idea of giving, not receiving. If all you're doing is trying to get attention, you're there for the wrong reasons. It's important to find a charity or organization that aligns with your own values, because it's a partnership that may become long-lasting, and that can only help you both in the long run.

As with business sponsorships, there may be several deciding factors in whom you decide to lend your support to. If you are marketing to a wide range of potential customers, you may wish to avoid nonprofits that are overly political in one way or another. That's a judgment call based solely on what your company is comfortable doing. Many charities advocate for one position or another, and if it's something you feel passionate about then definitely go for it! On the other hand, charities for things like children's hospitals, veterans' assistance, or helping stray animals tend to be less political and polarizing, and may be a better choice if your marketing is casting a wider net.

The benefits of charity association are most often very similar to those of business sponsorship (see pages 70–71), and a lot of the reasons listed there are relevant here, too. In addition, most charities hold regular fundraisers and events to bring in money for their work. If your budget can accommodate it, offer a matching grant of, say, up to $5,000 (or whatever is best for you). This doubles the amount of money they receive, and makes you memorable as a generous benefactor; everyone wins! Of course, you will have to determine if the Return on Investment (ROI) is worth that kind of investment, but if it's a cause that you already believe in, then you're doing good in the world, and that's what's most important. If money isn't an option, even offering pro bono sponsorship in the form of advertising and assistance or volunteer work can be a great way to build a new relationship, and will be much appreciated.

> **"You have not lived today until you have done something for someone who can never repay you."**
>
> **—JOHN BUNYAN**

DIRECT MAIL CAMPAIGNS

Direct mail may seem like another one of those marketing strategies that is outdated, and if not dead, it's at least looking antiquated and tired. This can be true, but there can also still be value in considering this form of marketing. It has some advantages: in the age of social media and random emails, direct mail can be way more targeted to specific groups, and it has a nice personal touch that the digital versions just don't. This is probably truer for companies whose customers are other companies and businesses, but if your customer base is small, you might be able to take advantage of some direct mailing. Here are some important points to remember.

- **Direct mail is still popular with recipients.**
Various studies have shown that nearly 75 percent of people actually prefer getting direct mail to yet more emails, and over half of people feel more valued if they receive mail personalized to them. It's something tangible, even if it's just a coupon or an offer for some other benefit. It can't be deleted and has real value in the real world. This can be a great opportunity for you to really hone in on who you value and nurture those relationships. And you can be as creative with your mailings as your imagination and budget allows. It's a chance to really stand out!

- **If you're reaching out to the public, direct mail can reach a larger demographic.** This is especially true if the older segment of the population is a part of your target audience. They're less likely to use emails or social media, but just about everyone goes to their mailbox.

- **But choose your recipients wisely.** Unless you have an enormous budget, sending out a brochure to 100,000 potential buyers in the general public, even if they are in your targets, is probably not going to be a good use of your funds. But a direct mail campaign to other businesses that need what you offer? Or maybe to people who are already on your mailing list to give them a gentle reminder that you still exist? Now you're talking! That personal touch might be just the thing to encourage them to buy, or bring them back.

- **Remember that direct mail isn't going to give you miraculous results.** Sending out 1,000 postcards in the mail will *not* get you 1,000 responses. Or 500. Or even 100. In fact, the cold hard truth is that response rates are low no matter what kind of method you use, and can be anywhere from 5–7 percent for physical mails. But the response rate for email marketing is often even lower than that (2–3 percent), so it's important to target your mailings very carefully.

- **Timing is everything, too.** Consider when you'll be sending out your mail. Direct mail is great at the holidays. Send out cards to your existing customers, maybe with a personal thank you for their business. Offer them a little gift, maybe a scan code that takes them to some exclusive content on your site or a preview of your next release. Or if you want to do something charitable, send them to a site that offers assistance to the needy and offer to make a matching donation to that charity, up to a certain amount. There are many ways to engage your customers during the season of giving!

- **Direct mail as a whole is declining, but that's actually good news!** With fewer and fewer people using it, when you decide to step up and send out that mailing, you're going to stand out! You won't get lost in the torrent of physical junk mail, because there's a little bit less of it every year, but you'll make an impression that a regular email won't.

PRESS RELEASES

A press release is simply an announcement to the media made by a person, or a company, or anyone, about something coming up that they want the world to know about. It could be an event, a product, or anything that gets the word out, but often it involves some sort of event at a specific date and time. If you company is releasing a new product, you'll probably be having some sort of public unveiling, and you'll want as many people as possible to attend. The press release is a good way of letting them know about it.

- **Press releases might be as short as a simple calendar listing (for a concert or a talk), or they might be a few paragraphs long, giving far greater details.** It's not uncommon to include two versions in the same release so that media outlets can choose which one they want to run. Print media will tend

to favor short press releases for calendar listings, because their space is limited, but online publications may allow you to stretch out a bit and tell your readers a bit more about the next big thing you're revealing to them.

- **Various news media will be your main targets for these releases.** This can include daily newspapers, weekly circulations, or even monthly publications, both in print and online. The best part is, there is often no cost to send releases to these outlets, though they will have deadlines, especially if the release concerns an event. For a daily publication, you may be able to leave sending it out until shortly before the event, but weeklies and monthlies will almost certainly want your press release long before the date in question. You'll have to check with each publication to find out their specific guidelines.

- **Wading through a pile of potential papers and periodicals can seem like a slog, but once you've done it, you won't need to change much for your future press releases.** Unless something new happens, such as a listing editor leaving or policy changes, or some similar shift, the process is the same each time. If you have a big release that needs to go out to a large number of periodicals, it can get tedious to have to email each one out to each address, but this can be automated, and there are even services that will do it for you, often for a low cost. This can actually be quite useful, because they will keep up to date on who and where to send information. All you'll need to do is provide your press release to them at the appropriate time.

[

"When people are talking about you, answer them."

—ANDY SERNOVITZ

]

FLYERS AND BROCHURES

Like direct mail, many people wonder if these more low-tech forms of getting the word out actually still work and if they're even relevant these days. Once again, the answer is yes, with certain qualifications. Now more than ever, you have to target your market carefully and only distribute flyers to those who might actually be interested in what you offer. Otherwise, you're just wasting paper and money. There are two kinds of flyers: mailed and door drops, and it should be pretty obvious what each one is. Your company budget will determine how many you choose to print up and what your distribution process will be like.

- **Mailed flyers:** Mailed flyers still do surprisingly well. As a form of direct mail (see pages 75–76), they can be targeted to specific audiences or areas, and it's estimated that more than half of all these pieces of paper are at least looked at by the person receiving them; that's actually a good number! Even if they choose not to act on it right away, they may save it for a later date (especially if some offer is made, such as a discount).

- **Door drops:** These are most useful for local businesses serving neighborhoods: coffee shops, pizza and other take-out services, auto repair, salons, local bookshops, fitness centers, etc. They're also great if you're advertising your sponsorship of a local event. If your business is frequented by a local population, door drops might be a very good way to engage with them, especially if you are just opening. You can include discounts and coupons, either on the flyer itself or accessible by a download code. There isn't much targeted marketing that goes into these campaigns. Perhaps you just choose the thousand nearest homes to your business and drop off a flyer or brochure at the front door of each. The problem, of course, is that this can be time-consuming, and you'll have to pound the pavement and get out there to get your message out (or hire someone to do it for you, if you're feeling lazy!). On the plus side, it's a chance to see more of your neighborhood, see what other businesses are out there, and get some exercise!

Whether mailed or dropped off, your flyer should have certain key things about it:

- **Be well designed.** OK, be honest with yourself. If you don't have the skills to do a good graphic design, hire someone to do it right. You want to make a great first impression, and if your flyer is filled with clunky, low-res images or mistakes in alignment, people will notice. Keep it simple, and get it done right the first time.

- **Be brief and to the point.** No one wants an essay on a piece of paper. Modern attention spans are simply too short. Decide on the main message for this flyer and stick to it. Are you offering a discount or coupon? Is it time-sensitive? Then focus on that. Your readers don't want the history of your business or multiple messages.

- **Invest in proper printing.** Full-color printing will make the best impression, but even if it's black and white, don't just run down to your local copier shop and run off a bunch of copies. Again, you want to impress, so show your potential customers that you take your business seriously. Having it look good will pay off in the long ruin.

- **Include all of your contact information.**
This should go without saying, but websites, phone numbers, and a physical address (if you have one) are essential. Scan codes that let people jump right to your site or online offer with their phones are great, too! This  will give you a good idea of how many people responded to the flyer, and whether this kind of campaign is worth using in the future.

PUBLIC ADS AND BILLBOARDS

Again, you might think that billboard advertising has gone the way of the dodo, but it simply isn't so. With the rise of digital and animated billboard technology (think *Blade Runner*), billboards are enjoying a big resurgence as a kind of grand display tactic that (at least for a few moments) gets people's attention off their phones. And they're not just big signs on buildings or along freeways either. Bus stops now have digital ad screens, and busses have long advertised all kinds of things on their sides. Cars are starting to drive around with digital ad screens attached to the tops of their roofs; the driver gets a small percentage of the ad cost for agreeing to go about with it on their car.

Whether you agree with this kind of advertising or not, it's out there, and research proves that it's only going to get bigger in the coming years; studies have shown that using so-called outdoor ads is the fastest growing method for advertising and marketing aside from the internet; these ads now rank fourth globally behind the internet, television, and newspapers. And it's not just ads on screens; even good old-fashioned single images are enjoying a comeback. So, is billboard advertising for you? It may be, but you have a few important things to consider.

- **Does your budget allow for this kind of expense?**
  A well-placed ad in front of potentially tens of thousands of people a day is not going to be cheap. If your budget or prospects are modest, you'll have to consider whether this is a good use of your funds.

- **Is the proposed location right for the kind of audience you want to reach?** Again, your target markets are crucial for deciding when and where to place your ad. If it's for an upcoming event, then ads in the vicinity and around the time of the event are the obvious choice. If it's for a service or a product that isn't time-specific, you'll have to be more careful about the time and place to maximize the ad's effectiveness.

- **Repetition can be both good and bad.** If your sign is in a place where large amounts of people can see it every day, that's good! But if your sign is in a place where large amounts of the *same* people can see it every day (like on a commute route), there's the risk that they're eventually just going to tune it out and may even start to feel negatively about it if it doesn't go away. Plus, if there was something they didn't like about it to begin with (and you have no control over that), they're going to like it even less after two weeks of having to look at it daily. Think about the times this has happened to you. Unfortunately, it's a risk you'll have to take.

- **Understand targeting of users.** It may seem Orwellian, but larger companies are already tracking potential customers by their phone usage and other data to determine where to place ads that will be most effective. It already happens all the time on the internet (unless you have no-tracking software installed), and it's become a thing in the real world as well. Whether or not you approve of this kind of behavior, it's now a part of the advertising landscape.

- **You'll usually be locked in to a set amount of time for your ad.** This can vary, but might be up to three months or more. And you have to pay for all that time, even if you don't use all of it, or you find out that the ad is a failure and want to withdraw it. You need to be very sure about your product, service, or event before you go for outside advertising. If in doubt, start small, and test the reactions.

[CHAPTER 4:]

MARKETING AND ADVERTISING USING SOCIAL MEDIA AND THE INTERNET

There's no denying it; the internet is essential to your success. You simply cannot compete or make yourself known in today's business world without a strong internet presence. Marketing using the internet is its own thing and is very different from traditional marketing, though many of the underlying ideas are the same. This chapter covers the basics of what you need to know and do, from websites to social media, to blogs and other forms of online communication. Don't delay in getting on with these or skip over them with the idea of coming back later. The online portion of marketing is so important that your website and social media accounts need to be in place right from the start to give you the best chance of having your message heard and reaching the right people.

TYPES OF INTERNET MARKETING

Marketing on the internet has many of the same principles and ideas as old-fashioned marketing, but the internet allows for a much greater reach and the possibility to have a huge impact. Here is a rundown of some of the many options you can use to market and promote. Not everything will be suitable for your business, and you may find that some methods work better than others. But you should have more than enough to keep you busy on a regular basis as you promote and grow your business.

- **Content Marketing:** Content marketing is, simply put, providing useful information and other content to a potential audience that helps attract a loyal group of followers over time. It's not about selling your products or services. Rather it's about establishing yourself as an authority. A good example would be an investment firm that sends out a weekly newsletter with financial tips and news. They're not selling their services, but are instead providing free valuable information to investors, who then may choose to work with this firm because they've developed trust and a good relationship with them. The firm never tries to make a sale with this method; it just helps others make wise decisions. It's a great example of cultivating relationships by offering, rather than expecting. This kind of marketing is great for almost any industry, and you can tailor it to your specific offerings and targets.

- **Affiliate Marketing:** Affiliate marketing is allowing others to market and sell for you. The idea is that you allow others to advertise your product and for each sale they make (or maybe each visit to your site via theirs), they get a small commission. The more business they bring to you, the more they make, and the more you make. Everybody wins! In theory, at least. Some people get into affiliate marketing to advertise others' products, thinking they'll become millionaires through passive income. Does it happen? Sometimes, but it's not that common. As a business, it can be a good way to get the word out about your new product.

- **Newsletters and Mailing Lists:** If you don't have a newsletter, you should. It's a great way to keep interested prospects up to date with what you're doing. The simplest way to set up an email mailing list is to have the option available on your site. Remember that most people get enough emails as it is, so you're going to need to give them a good reason to give you their address. How do you do that? By offering some kind of free content in exchange. This could be a report, a video, or a link to more information. It's something that's only available once they sign up. But it needs to be something of value; a one-page PDF is not likely to entice many people, but a free fifteen-page e-book just might. You have to be prepared to give something to get something, and this kind of enticement is a great way to show your generosity and that you're willing to offer them something more than a sales pitch. Remember that all email list programs require you to have an opt-out button, so that if someone doesn't want to receive your mails anymore they can leave. This is non-negotiable; if someone wants to move on, let them.

- **Blogging:** Your website would do well to have a blog that you keep updated regularly. Blogs should offer advice, insights, industry trends, articles of interest, and much more, but shouldn't be focused on what you do or sell. You want to give subscribers a chance to receive interesting new content that will keep them coming back for more. Decide on a regular schedule for your blog (once a week or more) and stick to it. If you don't consider yourself a great writer, hire someone who is. Blogs don't have to be long. A few paragraphs are enough to keep interest and engagement. It's the quality of the content that matters, and overly long blogs are not likely to be read by most people anyway. Be sure to advertise your blog on your other social media and encourage followers to subscribe. Include content there that's not available elsewhere, so that regular readers are rewarded by coming back again and again.

- **Search Engine Optimization (SEO):** SEO is all the rage right now, and with good reason. By using the correct keywords, you can get your website and other online material up to the top of search engine results. This is critical for getting your message out. In an online world where everyone is climbing over everyone else to be noticed, you have to stand out. Having a webmaster or writer that can get your pages into the top results is more than a worthwhile investment, and will give you a much-needed boost in the shouting match. SEO is a bit of a complex subject, but you need to learn about it and take it seriously.

- **Using Influencers:** Does someone famous use your product or service and like it? Awesome! Are they willing to tell their fans and followers about it? Even better! This can be a gold mine of free advertising and give you the kind of social proof that you can't buy. If you learn that such an individual is already happy with your product, try reaching out to them to see if they would be willing to spread the word (directly, or through an agent or manager, if they have one) on their social media pages. Some of them might want at least some compensation for this; if they were doing a television or radio ad, they'd certainly be paid for it, for example. You have to decide what your budget is and if this is worth the cost. A famous hockey star might be beyond your range, but a YouTube personality or Instagram influencer might not. If they have followers who are in your target market, it could be a great match!

- **Paid Advertising, the Pros and Cons:** Just like everywhere else, the internet is filled with ads. And mostly, it seems like people hate them. Ad blockers are common, because people want to see as few advertisements as possible when online. So, is paid advertising worth it, or are you just pissing off people? The answer is a definite maybe. Ads can work, but as with everything else, you have to be strategic, understand your exact target audience, and not go in with high expectations. Also, ads can run up costs very quickly if you don't watch it.

You have many ad options, such as paid search advertising (where you pay Google or other search engines to appear at the top of searches), paid social media advertising (paying for prominent spaces in a target market's feed on say, Facebook or Twitter), native advertising (sponsored articles and posts that are placed in the regular cycle of a site's output, so that they don't come across as ads), and display ads (the often hated ads that you click to take you to another site). All of these can work, but you'll need to do a lot of background research to see what's best for you. Just remember that various studies have shown that large majorities of users don't click any online ads, and most people find targeted ads that are based on their social media and browsing habits intrusive, annoying, and even creepy. Tread carefully.

- **Podcasts:** A podcast is a potentially fantastic way to market your business. You basically have three options: you can advertise on an existing podcast that reaches one of your target demographics, giving you a built-in audience that might be interested in your business. You can offer to be a guest on one or more podcasts, giving you the chance to speak about yourself and offer value to listeners. Or (and potentially best of all), you can start your own podcast and deliver value directly to your targets in a way similar to content marketing. With this option, you have complete control over the narrative, and as you build up an audience of listeners, you can grow with them and respond and react to what they want. You can have weekly (or more) chats about industry trends and interesting news, you can host special guests of your own, and you can solicit listener input, all while positioning yourself as a company in the middle of it all and never having to actively sell. Several companies such as Google, Apple, and Libsyn offer software to get you started, and once you're ready, you can make use of cross-platform marketing on your social media sites and elsewhere to bring in listeners.

- **Webinars:** Webinars give you the chance to offer instructional sessions that are actually a form of content marketing. If you are launching a new product, a webinar could be a great place to demonstrate it, for example. But what you want to be doing, as always, is giving a solution to a problem, not selling yourself. Nobody wants an infomercial. Keep it instructional and helpful. Focus on a single topic and limit the session to about forty-five minutes, allowing a quarter of an hour for questions afterward; it's important to engage your listeners and encourage their participation. As with podcasts and other media, it's very important to make some noise about the event on your social media pages, mailing lists, and elsewhere. Be mindful of time zones, and be very clear about when the webinar starts in which zone. Consider offering a replay for those who can't tune in or who miss it live. Regular webinars, like regular podcasts, can build up your reputation as a knowledgeable source, while also allowing for networking possibilities through guests, round tables, and other forms of connecting.

"Advertising brings in customers, but word-of-mouth brings in the best customers."

—JONAH BERGER

USING YOUR WEBSITE TO BEST ADVANTAGE

Your website is your online business card, brochure, and virtual company tour all rolled into one. Having a well-designed and accessible website is crucial for just about any business today, unless your company is well established and has a built-in clientele. Here are some points for how to take advantage of your online presence in your marketing efforts.

- **Take the time and invest in having it designed well.** Your website needs to be impressive. If it's outdated or hard to navigate, people won't stick around. Older websites are sometimes not well adapted for phones either, so make sure that's included in the layout. Users must have the same experience regardless of the platform they choose. There are countless good website templates out there that offer enticing designs and usability, so whatever you choose, make sure it's memorable and inviting. Your site needs to be easy to navigate and not confusing or frustrating. Lots of animations and auto-start videos can be off-putting (really, they can). The money and effort you spend on it now will come back to you many times over.

- **SEO rules all.** SEO is the hot topic these days. Everyone talks about it, everyone wants it, and every website designer offers it. SEO simply involves the use of the right keywords to make sure that when people are using search engines, your site comes up at the top of the searches. With everyone scrambling about and shouting "Notice me over here!" you need to be able to stand out. Research the keywords that are essential to your marketing message. If possible, see what words your competitors are using.

A variety of keywords are good, but you may want to narrow down the focus. Making them more specific will ensure that the right people come to you, since they already know what they want. The closer you can position yourself to their needs, the better.

- **Keep it current.** Your website should never be out of date. Ever. It's essential to always keep things like news and blogs up to date with regular posts. How often have you gone to a site and seen that the most recent post or update was, say, fourteen months ago? It happens all the time. And how much do you care about that site? Probably not much. On that note . . .

- **If you have a blog, use it.** Whether you write it yourself or have someone else do it, try to keep posting regularly, even if it's just a short update on what your business is doing, an interesting article about the industry, or something similar. Give people a reason to want to come back regularly.

- **Offer a free gift.** A download of some useful information (or a link to it) is a great way to entice visitors to your page. These are often done in exchange for the person's email. By signing up for your mailing list, they get something in return, and maybe the promise of more free content in the future. Just make sure that this content has real value, something they might even be willing to pay a little money for, only it's for free.

- **Make some pages shareable.** Do you have great content in your blogs, an article that's worth reading, an announcement about a free gift for new users? Make it easy to share that content online, especially to social media. Visitors that have a good experience may well want to tell others about it, and if you let them do so with ease, you're basically letting them market for you. This is good social proof and online word of mouth.

- **Make all the information on your site valuable.** Tell visitors about your product or service in a clear way and make sure to leave nothing out, but don't overwhelm them. Likewise, if you have good reviews, endorsements, and testimonials, it can be good to sprinkle them about in strategic places. A little extra push from satisfied customers or clients is always a good thing.

- **Make it very easy for people to contact you.** How often have you gone to a site, and the contact link is hidden all the way at the bottom of the landing page, after a lot of scrolling? It's like they don't want even to talk to you, and, honestly, that's probably true in some cases. Don't be those people. Make your emails, phone numbers, and physical address (if you have one) easy to find.

> ## "Discoverability equals sales in the digital world."
>
> **—DEV CHANDAN**

SEO VERSUS SEM: WHAT'S THE DIFFERENCE?

You've probably heard of both of these terms, but you may not be sure of what they are or how they are different. They do overlap, but it's important to understand those differences and not use them interchangeably.

- **Search Engine Optimization (SEO):** SEO is a more organic way of increasing website traffic, using keywords that will help position the site at the top of the search. It's a part of a broader SEM strategy. When you put up your website, a search engine will "crawl" through it, scanning it to determine the quality of the content. The more relevant you can make it to the site's purpose, the more likely it will feature higher up in a search result. Your goal is to improve your **SERP** (Search Engine Results Page) so that your page comes up higher in the listings when someone is searching for what you offer. If you can eventually position yourself to be the first result, that's fantastic!

To improve your website's searching ranking, include these features:

- **Use selected keywords.** These words can be in the metadata (also known as off-page optimization), alt text, or the main part of the text the user sees, such as in headings and body text. Make sure that you use the words and phrases most closely related to what you offer. Do your research using Google Analytics, customer feedback, and even what words your competitors are using for insight into your own strategy (see below for a list of programs that can be very useful in finding the right keywords). However, **don't** just stuff the same few words in everywhere you can on your pages! Search engines tend to view this as a characteristic of spam sites, and you'll be penalized for it with a lower ranking.

- **Optimize your site for mobile use.** This is essential for businesses these days. Since more than ever people access the internet from their phones, your site has to be ready to be seen and used in this format. Having a phone-ready site can help improve your SERP ranking.

- **Optimize your site for voice searches.** Increasingly people are asking their phones to find what they're looking for. Nearly a third of all topics searched will be in this format after 2020. These types of queries will require you to input longer keywords and phrases, as people tend to ask questions such as "Where is a good place to get a great latte?" You'll need to anticipate what people might ask.

- **Review your off-page optimization.** Having good links is especially important in improving your optimization. A scan of your website that sees that it links to other reputable sites improves your own site's ranking. A links page and a blog can both very helpful for this.

- **Hire an SEO expert.** It's worth considering bringing in outside help for this work, because you want your rankings to be the best possible. An SEO copywriter or other SEO expert can review your site and recommend changes to improve your rankings.

- **Search Engine Marketing (SEM):** SEM is a broader approach that includes SEO. It involves using optimization and paid advertising on search engines to increase a site's visibility in searches. SEM is not just a form of paid search, however, since like SEO, paid advertising is a part of SEM. But because of the paid aspect of it, SEM can deliver results faster than an organic SEO strategy. By getting your ad placed prominently at the top of a keyword search, you'll get your site in front of a lot more users.

Some tips for successful SEM implementation:

- **Research the best keywords for you.** There are number of good programs to help you do this these days: Google Trends, SEMRush, Keywordtool.Io, SpyFu, and Google Ads Keyword Planner are all good. You'll have to investigate each to see which of these is the best option for your needs. You'll also need to think of your target markets and what they are likely to be searching for.

- **Create compelling ad copy.** This is essential. If you're not comfortable doing this yourself, hire an expert who is. The language of your ad will have a big impact on whether or not people click through to your site.

- **Understand the concept of pay-per-click (PPC).** PPC is pretty much what it sounds like: each time someone clicks on your ad and is taken to your site, you pay a small amount. You determine the amount beforehand, based on your budget. If a lot of people click your ad, you'll pay more, but the idea is that some of those visitors will eventually become customers or otherwise benefit you, so the ad pays for itself over time.

- **Set your budget and stick to it.** Knowing that you'll be paying for each click, you have to set a limit on how much you're willing to pay.

- **You'll need to enter an ad auction.** In order for your ad to be in the running to appear in as search engine result, you'll need to enter into an auction (**Google AdWords** and **Bing AdCenter** are two of the biggest ad sites, and the ones you'll probably be working with at first). This is not an auction in the classic sense. Rather, you will enter the keywords that you want to bid on. Then the search engine will make the determination about displaying your ad based on the amount you are willing to pay and something called your Quality Score.

- **Understand your Quality Score.** For Google, this score is an estimate based on the quality of your ad, the keywords you're using, how relevant the ad is to the searcher, and the quality of the landing page the ad takes the user to. For Bing, it's a measure of how competitive the ad is based on the keywords of your competitors. In both cases, the higher the number (between 1 and 10), the better.

- **Be aware that your ad won't always appear.** Even if you meet all the criteria, there are many reasons why it might not show up in every search related to your keywords.

- **Keep an eye on metrics to determine how well your ad is doing.** Some ads work great; some don't. You'll need to monitor the ad's success to see if this strategy is worth your investment. Data like impressions and click-through rates will be very important in determining the ad's effectiveness.

- **Recognize the importance of Amazon.** Amazon's search service now rivals Google's for potential shoppers. The advantage here is that people are already on the site to buy, which means they are a step closer to becoming your customer. Amazon's SEM works in a similar way to those of other search engines and is worth your time to investigate. Go to **advertising.amazon.ca** for all the details.

- **Understand that social media advertising is different.**
  Facebook, Twitter, and the like are a bit different, and some don't consider advertising with them to be true SEM. One of the best ways to describe their ads is that they help your audience find you when browsing through their feeds. Go to these sites for more details:

  - facebook.com/business/ads

  - business.twitter.com/en/solutions/twitter-ads.html

  - business.instagram.com/advertising

  - youtube.com/ads

  - forbusiness.snapchat.com

> **"Social media is about the people. Not about your business. Provide for the people and the people will provide for you."**
>
> **—MATT GOULART**

SOCIAL MEDIA DOS AND DON'TS

Social media, for better and worse, is here to stay. It has permanently changed not only business culture but society as well. Your business will almost certainly use some of the platforms listed below (and if it isn't using them, it should be). Only you can decide which ones are best for you. Remember, it's not necessary to have a presence on all of these sites, though some businesses do. It depends on your product or service and your target markets. With all of these possibilities, you'll want to spend time analyzing data to see what kind of interactions you're having—what's working and what isn't. Analytics are crucial to social media business success! Here are few basic guidelines for each service.

FACEBOOK

- **Do:** Use appropriate images for your page, such as a logo and related images. Make sure that your about page is fully filled out with a brief summary of who you are and what you do. Include all contact information. Respond promptly to all messages. Post regularly and be sure to advertise your Facebook page on your other media. Use Facebook's many tools to improve engagement. Share other relevant content that you're interested in and watch your analytics to see what kind of response you're getting.

- **Don't:** Turn your page into a sales pitch. No one wants to see you advertising your products every day. That will simply lead to people leaving your page, or at least unfollowing it. You're there to engage, not sell. Also, don't post things that are of no interest to your audience just for the sake of regular posting.

 # TWITTER

- **Do:** As with Facebook, choose images that reflect your business and include relevant contact information on your profile. Post regularly, preferably more than once a day. Share things that are interesting and complementary to your message. Hashtags are your friends on Twitter, but be careful about overdoing them. A few per post is fine. Keep link URLs short (there are any number of ways to do this) so that you don't eat up valuable character space. Engage with your followers; ask them questions. Use the pinned post option to keep an important post at the top.

- **Don't:** Retweet without commenting; tell your audience why they should be interested in what you're sharing. Don't post sloppy tweets with poor grammar and spelling; Twitter doesn't let you edit, so get it right the first time! Don't make your posts too lengthy: 280 characters should be plenty to say what you need to say. Longer threads won't really improve engagement or response. Definitely don't make every tweet about you.

 # YOUTUBE

- **Do:** If your business has a YouTube channel, understand what you are posting for; your target markets need to be well defined, since you're asking them for their time. Post regularly and make sure your videos are of good quality, both audio and video; professionalism always counts! Make sure that keywords match the video's content. Embed a link in the video back to your site or blog, so that viewers have the option of learning more. Consider creating playlists of similar, relevant videos. Take the time to respond to comments and questions.

- **Don't:** Create a YouTube channel just to have it; what's the goal? Don't obsess over your videos going viral; concentrate instead on building a steady, regular audience of subscribers. Be wary of overusing annotations in videos, since they can become annoying, so let the video content speak for itself. Don't post just to be posting; make sure the video has something meaningful to say.

INSTAGRAM

- **Do:** Have a regular posting schedule, whether every day, or every Tuesday and Thursday, or whatever is best for you. Try also to send posts out at the same time, based on your research as to the optimal times. Two posts a day is probably enough at the start. With Instagram, you can only provide one outside link in your bio, so make it count! This may change frequently. If you put up a post with more information available, direct viewers to your bio page with a simple message such as "Link in bio page." The goal here is to drive traffic to that external site. Hashtags rule on Instagram, and you're permitted a large number per post, so use them often and strategically.

- **Don't:** Randomly post images that are not relevant. Try to keep a theme going with your business. If you are having trouble coming up with meaningful posts daily, consider scaling it back for a while. A good, relevant post twice a week is much better than random musings every day.

 LINKEDIN

- **Do:** LinkedIn is a bit different from the preceding examples, and you'll want to make even more effort to present yourself professionally. Keep all information current, and treat your page like a marketing brochure. When you do update, turn off your notifications; people don't need to know you're updating. Be respectful and professional in groups, and only join those that are relevant to you. Remember that when you view someone's profile, they know, unless you change your settings to "anonymous" while browsing. You don't want to get a reputation as being creepy or stalker-ish.

- **Don't:** Don't spam, and don't try to connect without reaching out to the other person or company first. The generic "join my network" button gives others no reason at all to connect with you. Build relationships and the connections will come. Don't use your page to talk about only you (again, this is always true, everywhere).

SNAPCHAT

- **Do:** Snapchat isn't just for younger users sharing photos anymore. If your target demographic is in the age range of teenagers to mid-thirties, it might well be worth your time to have a presence here. Post often (a few times a day), since Snapchat posts only last for twenty-four hours. Be sure to let your followers on other social media platforms know about it! Create a sponsored filter or lens (the website has details). These can be really funny and engaging, and will make you stand out; humor is a great marketing tool on this site. Invite users to contribute by sending you their photos using your brand in some way; you can include these in your stories.

- **Don't:** Don't post overly long stories. Attention spans are short, and you don't want to be boring people and having them lose interest. Don't always rely on sound, especially for time-sensitive promotions. Many people might be viewing your Snap in public and don't have their sound on or their earbuds in; not everyone can listen in. Also, don't go too far off-brand from why you're here. If you're trying to engage a specific demographic, keep all posts relevant to them. Don't try to make your posts too perfect. Instead, be spontaneous and fun, and even allow for a little error to creep in; it makes your business more human and more relatable.

PINTEREST

- **Do:** Pinterest may seem like an unusual choice as a social media tool, but many businesses use it successfully, especially those that sell products. If you do your research and find that it's right for you, complete your profile with all the important information, with keywords that make your page more visible in searches. Make sure that the images you post are of good quality! The whole point of the site is the visuals, so poor pictures will do you no good at all. Pin regularly (preferably every day), and check out which group boards, if any, you'd like to participate in. Pin content other than your own; just make sure it's related to your business. You want to keep your pins fresh and interesting, and, as always, endless self-promotion will get you nowhere. Rich pins, which offer real-time information, are great for businesses that sell.

- **Don't:** Don't leave boards empty; it sends that message that you couldn't be bothered to fill them in. If that's the case, what else can't you be bothered to do? Also, don't pin everything to one board. Have different boards for different topics. Don't overdo it with the hashtags in your profile description; this isn't Instagram, and hashtags are used for searching, so the more focused you can make it, the better.

- **Other Social Media Options:** Platforms like WhatsApp and Messenger (both owned by Facebook) offer many possibilities for business. WhatsApp allows for business profiles, and Messenger is integrated into Facebook's larger platform, which is good news if you already have a Facebook page. WeChat, QQ, and Qzone are all based in China, and may well be worth your time to explore if you are interested in expanding your operations into China or East Asia. Also Asian-based, TikTok has a rapidly growing number of users and is especially popular with young people, but it's uncertain how valuable a tool for business it will be going forward. More social media platforms will keep appearing in the next few years, and it's well worth your time to keep an eye on trends and see what might be a good fit. Getting in on the ground floor of a new site or app may give your business a needed boost at some point, so be open to a rapidly changing social media environment!

[CHAPTER 5:]

MAKING THE
MOST OF EVENTS

Events of all kinds can really be your place to shine.
They are all about in-person and one-on-one meetings with
others and are a rich source of potential contacts, new friends,
colleagues, and customers. But you have to be smart and
go in with the right mindset. This section shows you how to
prepare and get the most out of any event, while presenting
yourself in a professional and respectful way that doesn't
scream "used-car salesman" to the people you meet. As the
old saying goes, you don't get a second chance to make a first
impression, and if you blow it at the first meeting, it will be
much harder to save your reputation later on. Marketing is all
about making the right kinds of connections, and there are all
kinds of events that can be the places to do it.

Depending on the focus of your business, some events may be better suited to you than others. This will require background research on your part to find the best fits for your business or company. Not everything out there will be a good match, even those events that at first seem like they might be great. Or you may attend a conference or show one year and find that it's really not for you. Be realistic and expect some disappointment. If it's an annual event, consider visiting it one year before actually signing up for it. There is a bit of trial and error to the process, and you'll only figure out what events suit you by dipping your toes in and going for it.

> **"Don't push people to where you want to be; meet them where they are."**
>
> **—MEGHAN KEANEY ANDERSON**

EVENTS OF ALL KINDS: TEN WAYS TO BE PREPARED!

> Whether you're at a conference, networking event, a product launch, a charity event, a benefit, or any other kind of gathering, there are several things you'll want to do beforehand to get ready. Going in without a plan will get you nowhere and could end up causing you problems later on. Here are some tips for being prepared, so you can go in with confidence and make the most of it.

1. **What do you want from this event?** The answer may seem obvious: you're hoping to network and meet new people, but it goes deeper than that. Remember always that you should be looking for ways that you can help others, not just trying to see what you can get from them. Are there specific people there you want to connect with? Have you identified a need in a certain sector or niche that you would be great at satisfying? Have specific goals in mind, but limit these to only a few, two or three at most, so you can concentrate your energy on them. If it's to make three new connections and make sure that your company is well represented in some way, that's just fine.

2. **Are there specific people you want to meet?** If so, take some time to find out a bit about them. Read their LinkedIn profile and/or their page on the company website (if they have one). Knowing a little bit about them isn't stalking; it's positioning yourself to be able to carry on a meaningful conversation. Telling them that you admire something they accomplished is a great conversation starter. It can even be a good idea to

reach out to specific people in advance to let them know you'd like to meet up with them. If this seems appropriate and not intrusive, it's fine to do.

3. **Consider helping out at the event.** Do they need volunteers? People to greet those coming in? Think about getting involved. If the event has name tags, be sure to wear yours! If someone is alone and looks lost, offer your help.

4. **Have your elevator pitch ready.** If someone does ask about your business or work, have your pitch ready. The elevator pitch is a brief description of who you are and what you do. It should always focus on the solutions you can bring, not on how great you are (even if you're really great!). Also, keep it short and sweet. Talk less and listen more.

5. **Be sincere and listen to others.** Following from the previous point, make sure you give each person your full attention and respect. Just think about how you want to be treated and act the same way. Listening to others with genuine enthusiasm for what they have to say builds trust and helps forge bonds. Go in ready to listen and learn.

6. **Dress nicely and appropriately.** This should go without saying, but dress according to the type of event it is. Casual? Black-tie? Somewhere in between? Make the effort to find out. Also, it never hurts to be a little bit overdressed.

7. **Have your business cards ready.** This is the place where you'll need them. See pages 43–44 for all you need to know about business cards but were afraid to ask.

8. **Be ready to collect others' business cards.** Have a designated place for storing them. Don't just stuff them into your pocket and assume you'll remember who each person was later. You won't. Also, in some cultures (especially in Asia), it's considered rude not to examine the card first and then put it in a special place. It's worth having a small notebook to jot down a few notes about the person you're talking with, so that when you follow up and connect with them again, you can have an email conversation that's meaningful. See pages 52–53.

9. **Turn your phone off or at least keep it put away.** You don't want a potentially useful meeting to be interrupted by calls and texts. Unless there is an emergency that you may need to tend to, you can skip having your phone on for a few hours. Really, you'll be fine.

10. **Always follow up after the event.** See pages 52–53 for more details.

YOU'RE NOT THERE TO MARKET!

Whatever the event, remember that you are not there to sell yourself, your company, or your services. If the event is a benefit, first and foremost, you should be there because you support the goals of that benefit. Seeking out these kinds of gatherings to surreptitiously market yourself is sleazy, and people will notice. Here are some things to watch out for, both in your own behavior and in others.

- **Don't sell yourself.** Again, this can't be stressed enough. If all you're doing is trying to meet as many people as possible with the goal of attracting clients or customers, you're doing it wrong. Three good contacts are far more valuable than twenty-five who don't care and won't remember you even if you do email them the next day. Don't just try to meet everyone there. Make each connection meaningful.

- **Don't dominate conversations.** Again, listen, don't interrupt (ever!), and be ready to learn. Nobody wants to hear you talk about your accomplishments and pat yourself on the back. If they're interested in something specific, they'll ask. Don't be overly loud, laugh too much or too hard . . . basically, just be polite and professional.

- **Don't name-drop.** On that note, it's unlikely that anyone cares about who you know, and you're not going to impress them by telling them. If you have a super famous celebrity as a client and it's actually relevant to what you're discussing, it may be OK to work it into a conversation, but if you lead with that kind of thing, it just presents you as bragging, boastful, maybe even shallow or desperate for attention.

- **Don't cling to people.** Have you met someone with whom you've clicked? Have you had a good conversation with someone who may open doors in the future? Congratulations! Now, leave them alone. They're not your new best friend, and they have things to do at the event that most definitely do not include you. If they circle around for another conversation later on, that's great! It means that you may well have made a meaningful connection. But give them space and don't be creepy. If the event has speakers, this is even more important. A lot of people will want to talk with them afterward, so don't hound them. This advice is especially true for events that aren't specifically for networking. If you're following around someone at a charity event, you might be asked to leave.

- **Watch your alcohol intake.** Seriously. If this is a benefit or a celebration, and wine or other alcoholic beverages are offered, be very careful about how much you imbibe, if you do drink. If you overindulge, you'll almost certainly do something you regret, make a bad impression, or otherwise cause disruption. Limit yourself to one drink, or, better yet, skip it altogether. You're not there to party.

WHY NON-NETWORKING EVENTS MAY BE BETTER FOR YOU

Honestly, a lot of people consider events that are marked as specifically for networking to be a waste of time. The problem is that everyone is going for the same reason, and the risk of everyone just circling about like vultures goes up greatly. Everyone is eyeing everyone else for potential leads and contacts, their business cards and pitches at the ready at a moment's notice to unleash on the masses, and is ultimately just trying to sell something to someone else. OK, this might be an exaggeration, but you can see how an event designated only for networking is going attract people of a different mindset than one that's more relaxed and social, or more geared for a common purpose. Networking events are more likely to bring out the kind of unsavory behaviors discussed in the previous section (see pages 106–7), and you'll find that you'll be fending them off as much as trying not to fall into those behavior traps yourself.

So what are some good alternatives to networking events that might feel lighter, less pressured, and allow for more spontaneity? Here are some suggestions.

- **Fundraisers for nonprofits and charities:** An event benefiting a charity that aligns with your values is an excellent place to meet like-minded people. Perhaps your company is even considering sponsoring or donating to the event (see pages 128–29), in which case, even better! People don't attend these benefits to sell things, and any conversations you have will feel more sincere and beneficial to everyone. Again, go in thinking about what you can contribute.

- **Food or wine-tasting events:** These can be great fun, and again, there may be room for your business to offer up some kind of sponsorship. Everyone loves good food and striking up casual conversations over a meal, so what's not to like? Influential people often attend these kinds of events, and if they are held on weekends, the feeling will be more relaxed and casual. If it's a wine tasting, just bear in mind the ever-prudent advice about taking it easy. Overindulging in this year's selection of fine Cabernets could get you in a lot of trouble without you realizing it until later!

- **Lectures and talks:** Is there an industry leader giving a talk in your town? Are there things you could learn from them (there probably are)? A talk can be a great place to absorb new information and ideas while having a chance to chat with like-minded people seeking the same knowledge. Just be mindful of the advice not to mob the speaker! An important note: the talk doesn't have to be about something in your industry; it literally can be about anything that you're interested in. You won't know who else might be attending until you go to a few and find out! Some of the best connections can be made seemingly randomly at unrelated events.

- **Volunteer work:** Related to charity events, but this involves you taking more of active role in helping out an organization, rather than just sponsoring a fundraiser once in a while. This is ideal if there is a cause you genuinely support, but understand that it will take up some of your time, and the ROI may be small, if you're only thinking in monetary terms. On the other hand, the ROI may be excellent if you value the time spent and know that it's for a good cause. And if you happen to meet some excellent people along the way, so much the better!

- **Entrepreneur and small business organizations:** If you have a small business, it may be worth checking these out. There could be one or more for your industry in your area (or at least in the region), and they often sponsor meetings and social events.

> **"Pulling a good network together takes effort, sincerity and time."**
>
> **—ALAN COLLINS**

PROFESSIONAL CONFERENCES

Conferences offer a great chance to meet with industry leaders and experts, hear speakers on topics you're interested in, and connect with others of like mind. They can also be confusing, exhausting, and leave you feeling lost. Here some things to keep in mind.

- **Review your goals for the conference.** What do you want for yourself or your company? How can you bring your own value? Remember, that you're there to make meaningful connections, so plan ahead for how to offer your help.

- **Research everyone that you'll be interested in hearing speak or at least connecting with.** This doesn't take a lot of work, and it's good to go in prepared. Check out their websites, LinkedIn pages, and so on, to get a sense of whom you'll be talking to, and what their interests and needs are.

- **Some conferences can be spread out over a wide area, so dress professionally but comfortably.** If you're wearing amazing-looking shoes that are hell to walk in after thirty minutes, you're going to be miserable for the rest of the day. Look good, but be comfortable!

- **Don't forget your phone/tablet/laptop and charger!** Seriously, don't. Bring whatever electronic devices you need. You won't be able to do much of anything without them.

- **Use the conference hashtag(s) when posting about it to social media.** This is a great way for others to find you, and for you to see who else is attending. You're actually advertising yourself, and it's a good way to send out a general invite for people with similar interests and goals to meet up. Post about the sessions you're attending, and check in to see what others are posting about.

- **Keep your business cards at the ready.** Obviously.

- **Ask lots of questions.** You're there to learn.

- **But don't stalk people.** Don't be creepy; don't be clingy. If you have the chance to meet someone important to you, use the time wisely, as there are probably many others that want to speak to them, as well. And don't be a fan. They're people, just like you, and the more human your connection can be, the better.

- **Be prepared to take notes at talks, either by computer or by hand.** The talks you'll be attending will have a lot of valuable information. There are apps that can convert your handwriting into printed text, if you prefer to take notes the old-fashioned way. If it's allowed (and this will vary from conference to conference, and even session to session), you may be able to take photos of key slides and displays at talks, but always check first!

- **Budget your time.** You're not going to be able to see everything or attend every talk. You're better off getting in to hear two or three good talks than staying for only part of one and then having to dash off to something else. Prioritize and pick the sessions and events that you know you're going to get the most out of. If you're running around all day, you'll be exhausted by evening and no good to anyone if they want to socialize. In short, pace yourself!

- **Who is paying for you to attend?** Are you funding this yourself? Be mindful of your budget, as expenses can pile up quickly, especially if you're going out for drinks or buying lunch/dinner for new friends every day. If your company is paying for you to be there, you'll need to keep a running tab of reasonable expenses. You may be entitled to compensation, but they probably won't pay for everything! Check with your employer to find out what their policy is.

[
"Content is king."
—*BILL GATES*
]

TRADE SHOWS

Trade shows and conferences often overlap; both may have talks and presentations, and be great chances to meet leading people in your industry. They may even be called the same thing or have aspects of both melded into one big event. Trade shows have some differences, of course, with booths and showcase displays being a major feature. If you're attending a trade show, much of the advice for conferences applies. Here are a few extra things to keep in mind as you wander around, looking at every company's booth. Or maybe you're on staff at a company booth.

- **Outline what your company's goals are if you are presenting/have a booth.** Why are you there? What do you want to achieve? This could be any number of reasons: trying to attract new customers, trying to interest investors, getting the word out about a product launch, growing your mailing list and social media presence, attracting media attention, and much more. These goals will often overlap, but it's good to have a clear idea of what you want.

- **Choose the right shows.** This may seem obvious, but it's important to choose your potential shows wisely. Don't waste company time and money on events that won't put you in front of potential target markets. Also, take time to research each event and make sure that they are legitimate and well-run. There are any number of events that are a mess or even scammy. Does the event have a good website and a strong social media presence? Will they have good guests? Can you contact them, and do they respond? Be sure that the show you're interested in is on the level.

- **What is your budget?** If you're renting space, what will it cost? Do you need a big booth or a smaller one? How much can you afford to deck it out to make a good impression? It's worth investing in good signage (and the show may have regulations about what you can use), since it can be used again and again in the future.

- **Have your promotional material ready and looking top-notch.** Brochures, flyers, samples, coffee mugs, tote bags . . . whatever you've brought, make it look good and present it well. You want your brand to be memorable, so make sure it's looking its best.

- **Who among your competitors will be there?** And what will they be offering? Can you do better? Do they have bigger or more impressive booths? Are those booths located in better locations than yours? Can you make an impression that will stand out?

- **Consider breaking some news to the media.** If you have an upcoming announcement, a show is the perfect place to get it out there. Media is already in attendance and may want to hear what you have to say. Most shows have a media list. Ask them for it, and make sure to let the media know you have something big to say!

- **Send out a press release, both for your attendance at the show and if you have something important to announce.** You can also make great use of social media and mailing lists to announce that you're going to announce something! Once the news is out there, be sure to get it up on your social media platforms as soon as possible, so that those not attending can hear it, too!

- **Use social media extensively while you're there.** Not just to talk about yourself, but also other things that interest you, great new products and services, etc. As always, pay it forward. Spread the news about the good things others are doing, and give them good press.

- **Take tons of photos, both of your own booth and of the show in general.** Get photos of people (with their permission, of course!), especially if they are influential and like what you do. Getting peer and celebrity endorsements is always a great thing. Offer to do the same for others. As always, post extensively to social media as it happens.

- **Many booths will offer freebies and samples, so have something to carry them in.** If you're out wandering, having a "swag bag" is important while you're cruising around checking out potential contacts and competitors. Even if it's just paper material (such as brochures), you'll need something to carry it all in, so you're not struggling with an armload of paper, mugs, and baseball caps after an hour! Gather as much information as you can, including from your competition; it will help you sharpen and define your own message going forward.

- **Be sure to follow up.** Once again, this is critical. Follow up with everyone you met, whether industry contacts, media representatives, or celebrities and influencers. They all matter! Hand those business cards out to them and get on with follow-up emails. If you made contact with a genuine celebrity, try reaching out to that person's agent and seeing if you can follow up. You might be surprised at how many are willing to give you some more of their time.

- **Analyze the overall results and prepare to do it again.** Some shows will be fantastic, others not so much. Be honest about your results. Many shows are annual and it might be worth attending them every year, but some may just not be for you. Or maybe it was just an off year. Only you and your company will be able to determine if that show or shows in general are for you, but it's always worth trying at least once.

ROUND TABLE EVENTS

Round table events are a great chance to hear and be heard. Unlike conferences and trade shows, round table events are small, intimate, and offer a great opportunity to get to know others a bit more in-depth. In fact, they are often a featured component of a larger conference, and allow a smaller group of people to get more in-depth into a problem or issue—or just have a general discussion and propose solutions and strategies. These meetings often have no more than twenty people or so (sometimes a lot less) and can last for ninety minutes to two hours. Generally, the shorter the time period for the discussion, the fewer people should be there, in order to give everyone a chance to contribute fully.

If you are invited to one or have the chance to sign up for a relevant one at a bigger event, do it! They are a fantastic chance to meet new people and forge new connections, while working together as a team on solving a problem. Whether you're attending or hosting, here are some important things to keep in mind.

If you are attending:

- **Round table discussions are just that: discussions.** You're there to learn as much as speak, so give everyone proper attention and time. Input tends to be democratic rather than focused on one presenter or speaker, and that's the whole point, though they usually have a moderator who directs the flow of the meeting.

- **Be prepared to listen and take copious notes.** Your opinion matters, but so does everyone else's. You'll probably be delighted and surprised by the insights your colleagues bring and the answers they propose, so go in ready to absorb it all.

If you are hosting:

- **If you are the moderator or organizer, define your goals.** Why are you meeting? What do you hope to achieve? What is the agenda for the meeting? It's important to keep the discussion on track. It's easy to go off on tangents, but these eat up time quickly, so you'll have to be strict about keeping people on topic. On that note . . .

- **Keep your agenda small and focused.** You're there to work on a specific problem or topic, and you want the best input on it. Don't overwhelm your participants with too many issues all at once—save other issues for later round tables.

- **Have an agenda to hand out or email to everyone ahead of time.** This will further help keep the meeting focused. Include all of the points and important information you wish to bounce around, as well as start and stop times, and any other relevant information.

- **Establish the procedure, if necessary.** Does each person get a certain amount of time to speak before handing it over to someone else? Is there an order for who talks? Establish anything that you feel is necessary for the meeting to flow and stick to it.

- **Consider recording the conversation and having it transcribed.** If the attendees are open to the idea, it could be a valuable record of the meeting. Ideas that sometimes get lost in the process of note-taking will be better preserved for future reference. Just be sure to ask everyone's permission.

- **Follow up with results.** Did their ideas and suggestions work? Let them know! Keeping in touch with people is a great way to keep the conversation going. More round tables may come from this one, and you'll be on your way to building some strong and lasting relationships.

> **"The single greatest 'people skill' is a highly developed and authentic interest in the other person."**
>
> **—BOB BURG**

ENTREPRENEURIAL EVENTS

Depending on the size of your company, there are various events for small businesses and entrepreneurs that may be worth your time. These might be local gatherings (and they may occur regularly), or they might be more regional or even national. Many of these bigger events are in the form of industry conferences and similar gatherings, so the same rules apply here for what you should do to prepare and how to conduct yourself as you would at a more general conference.

Some entrepreneurial events may be focused on networking, which sounds good at first but actually can be problematic, since everyone is there to schmooze (see page 109). Or they may be educational gatherings, which are more beneficial. People attend to learn new things, and you'll have a better chance of making meaningful connections in this environment than at an event where everyone is trying to sell something to you. Larger isn't always better, and keeping your focus small and even local can really pay off.

Check your local listings to see what kinds of events might be happening near you.

INDUSTRY-SPECIFIC TALKS AND MEETUPS

Is someone well-known or positioned in your industry giving a talk in your town? Go! This is a great opportunity to meet up with like-minded individuals, and maybe get a small amount of one-on-one time with the speaker (but be mindful of the advice already given and don't hog their time!). Local and regional meetups like this tend to be less formal. They might have snacks and drinks and give you the opportunity to chat with others. If you can attend one or more of these, keep the following things in mind.

- **As always, go in with the idea that you are looking to create connections, not sell anything.** Don't be that person trying to leverage themselves with everyone in attendance.

- **Have your business cards ready.** But use them wisely. Don't hand them out like candy; be strategic.

- **Do introduce yourself to the speaker.** It's fine to go up for a quick chat. But keep it brief, and don't start spewing out everything about you or your company. This person is unlikely to be able to magically open a bunch of doors for you, so don't treat them that way. They're not there to give you a helping hand.

- **Do introduce yourself to others.** This is a great chance to meet your peers, and share stories and ideas. Give them the courtesy you would expect, and see what kinds of connections you can make. Be sure to follow up and get in touch after the talk!

- **Listen and ask questions.** Take a genuine interest in what others have to say. That way, when it's your turn to speak, you'll have their attention. Listen for what questions others might ask of the speaker, since someone may have a question or situation you hadn't thought of.

> **"Content is king, but engagement is queen, and the lady rules the house!"**
>
> **—MARI SMITH**

GET INVOLVED WITH COMMUNITY SERVICE GROUP EVENTS

If you volunteer, these can be a great place to get in touch with others. Working together on a common goal for an issue you feel passionate about is a fantastic way to form lasting bonds. As always, it's never about using people to get ahead, but you may find there are many people of like mind who you can help and in return might help you at some point. There may already be several of these kinds of events ongoing in your area, but you and your company can also consider sponsoring your own. Here are some ideas for events and activities you could host.

- **Help a local park or nature area:** Consider partnering with your city or town to help maintain and clean your green common areas.

- **Host an animal adoption day:** Come on, it's for puppies and kittens. What else do you need to say?

- **Support relief charities:** There are many different organizations giving aid to victims of natural disasters and other calamities around the world. Organize a drive to collect donations for the one of your choice.

- **Support your local public library system:** Libraries offer so much more than just books and are an invaluable presence in every community. Even just raising awareness about them is a big help. Fortunately, almost two-thirds of Canadians have library cards (which is comparable to the number who have passports), so a drive to support your library will probably be well received.

- **Host holiday a toy drive.** Or partner with an existing organization. Helping deliver holiday cheer to needy children is a wonderful way to give something back to the most vulnerable in your community.

- **Partner with a program for disadvantaged children.** There are undoubtedly organizations focusing on education, poverty, and lending a helping hand to those in need.

- **Encourage young people to vote.** This doesn't have to be a partisan issue, just an invitation to up-and-coming voters to be more involved in the political process, whatever their views.

- **Host a career day.** Whether at a school or as a separate event, invite key speakers and counselors to give advice for teenagers on what paths are open to them.

Obviously, these are just a few suggestions, but the possibilities are almost limitless!

CASUAL GET-TOGETHERS

> Networking breakfasts, lunches, and dinners,
> happy hours, days out, and much more—there's no
> shortage of casual get-togethers and fun activities
> that are great chances to meet up with others in a
> nonbusiness and nonpressured environment. As
> the attendee or the host, these events can provide a
> great opportunity to get away from work and just
> be yourself (within reason, of course). Here are
> few ideas.

- **Food gatherings:** No matter the time of day, everyone
  likes to eat! Breaking bread (or its gluten-free equivalents)
  can be a wonderful way to share stories and conversation
  with new people. Depending on how the meal is organized,
  you may even partner up with one or two individuals at
  first, and then be encouraged to move around. If alcohol is
  involved, watch what you do (see below).

- **Happy hour:** In principle, these can be good times to
  relax, unwind, and get to know others in a casual setting.
  A few things to remember, though: you're not required to
  drink. If you don't drink alcohol or just prefer not to on this
  occasion, that's fine. Simply state that fact and let it go. If
  anyone pressures you about it, that's rude and uncalled-for,
  but it also gives you a helpful red flag about how they might behave at
  other times. If you do drink alcohol at a happy-hour event, be careful about
  the amount and know your limits! You don't want to say or do something
  you'll regret later on.

- **Coffee:** Or whatever beverage one prefers. Like a meal with less food, or a happy hour without the alcohol. Regular coffee meetups are a wonderful idea.

- **Outdoor sporting events:** Are you into hiking? Climbing? Biking? Kayaking? There is no shortage of amazing opportunities to get outdoors and a huge variety of clubs and organizations all across Canada dedicated to them. Your business could easily book something though one of these groups and arrange a special event, inviting people whom you'd like to connect with. This will take a bit of background research, obviously, and not everyone will be willing or able to participate, but this kind of intensity will let you bond with others over a common interest that has nothing to do with your business, and that's always a great thing for future work.

- **Other sporting events:** Hockey, football, or whatever you can imagine can be an ideal chance to get people together from different places and see how they get on.

- **Cultural events:** Concerts, exhibits, art galleries, walking tours . . . there are so many ways for a group to meet up and have a good time. These may not seem like obvious choices, but remember, the goal here is not marketing or even networking; it's about making valuable connections that may eventually open doors.

CHARITY EVENTS AND FUNDRAISERS

> Supporting causes you believe in is appropriate at all levels of your business, from a one-person project to a large corporation. As with community service projects, it's a great way to get involved, get your community involved, meet great new people, and give something back. As the attendee or supporting business, you'll have the satisfaction of knowing that you're doing work for a good cause, while having the chance to reach out to new people and organizations.

If you are supporting the event, your business may be one of several cosponsors, or you may be the sole sponsor. Either way, the charity will probably already have its own goals defined: a fundraising amount, prizes given out, how to accept donations, and so on. All you'll likely have to do is plug into their existing structure. Here are some ideas for how you can assist in making the event a success.

- **Use your own advertising structures:** Your social media followers, mailing lists, and target audiences are already in place, so be sure to let them know about the event. Send out a press release, tweet about it, link to the charity's website, etc. There are many ways for you to raise the profile of the fundraiser that will cost you nothing but a bit of time—time that will be well spent in helping them out. Reach out to your colleagues and even to your competitors and let them know what's happening.

- **Offer your help with organizing and creating a theme:** Would a specific theme work for this fundraiser? Do you have ideas about what it could be? More often than not, just saying "give to this worthy organization" is not going to get people very excited; people and organizations ask for money all the time. So how can you make this event stand out? A raffle for prizes? A singles' night? A networking event? Any ideas you have will only help them. Maybe you know of a great space that can be rented at low cost, or can offer space in your own office (assuming it's big enough).

- **Be present on the day:** Sponsorship usually allows you to have a presence at the event, whether that's having a booth, a table, or some other way that lets attendees know about you. Whatever you decide in advance with the charity, take full advantage of it, but just remember that this is their time, and the focus should be on them. Even so, you can still be involved. Are they having a raffle? Can you offer one of your products as a prize? That's a great option! Is there some small token you can give to each guest (a mug, a bag, a USB stick with links to your site and its work with the charity)? There are ways to be memorable without being intrusive. Brainstorm with the charity and see what they'd like.

> **"Success isn't about how much money you make; it's about the difference you make in people's lives."**
>
> **—MICHELLE OBAMA**

RESOURCES

Every attempt has been made to provide a quality
and up-to-date introduction to the kinds of marketing
information. If you would like to dive much deeper into the
subject (and yes, you should go for it, because there are so many
interesting things to learn!), the following books and websites
will be amazingly helpful.

FURTHER READING

Here is a selection of books that go much more in-depth about many of the topics covered in this book. It's well worth investing some extra time and money in these works to get a thorough understanding of the marketing process, plus lots of great additional ideas and information.

Jonah Berger, *Contagious: Why Things Catch On* (Simon & Schuster, 2013).

Allan Dib, *The 1-Page Marketing Plan: Get New Customers, Make More Money, and Stand Out From The Crowd* (Page Two, 2018).

Seth Godin, *This Is Marketing: You Can't Be Seen Until You Learn to See* (Portfolio, 2018).

Brendan Kane, *One Million Followers: How I Built a Massive Social Following in 30 Days* (BenBella Books, 2018).

Dan S. Kennedy, *Magnetic Marketing: How To Attract A Flood of New Customers That Pay, Stay, and Refer* (Forbes Books, 2018).

Lonny Kocina, *The CEO's Guide to Marketing: The Book Every Marketer Should Read Before Their Boss Does* (Maple Island, 2017).

Andrew Macarthy, *500 Social Media Marketing Tips: Essential Advice, Hints and Strategy for Business: Facebook, Twitter, Pinterest, Google+, YouTube, Instagram, LinkedIn, and More!* (Independently published, 2018).

Jason McDonald, *The Marketing Book: A Marketing Plan for Your Business Made Easy via Think / Do / Measure*, 2020 Edition (Independently published, 2019).

Donald Miller, *Building a Story Brand: Clarify Your Message So Customers Will Listen* (HarperCollins Leadership, 2017).

Al Ries and Jack Trout, *The 22 Immutable Laws of Marketing: Violate Them at Your Own Risk!* (Harper Business, 1994).

Mark W. Schaefer, *Marketing Rebellion: The Most Human Company Wins* (Schaefer Marketing Solutions, 2019).

Dan Schawbel, *Promote Yourself: The New Rules for Career Success* (St. Martin's Griffin, 2014).

David Meerman Scott, *The New Rules of Marketing and* PR, 6th edition (John Wiley, 2018).

ONLINE RESOURCES

Here is a list of websites that offer much more detail on specific topics related to many aspects of marketing. These sites will allow you to go further in-depth when doing your marketing research. They offer a wealth of information on just about any topic you'll need to look into and valuable help where you need it.

Advertising Age

A subscription-based online publication that's all about the advertising world: trends, how-tos, current issues, and so on. If your business is the right size, this site may well be worth investing in.

adage.com

Adweek

Also a site by subscription, and filled with excellent articles on news, marketing, advertising, using digital tools, and much more. Again, if your business is at the right place and your budget allows for it, this might be worth your money.

adweek.com

The Association of Canadian Advertisers

Though it's a membership association for marketers and advertisers, the site has a lot of good free content in the form of articles and news on trends, talks, and other marketing-related topics.

acaweb.ca

Canadian Chamber of Commerce

From their website: "With a network of over 450 chambers of commerce and boards of trade, representing 200,000 businesses of all sizes in all sectors of the economy and in all regions, we are the largest business association in Canada, and the country's most influential." This site is an obvious choice when learning about the state of business in Canada, particularly how laws may affect you.

chamber.ca

Canadian Federation of Independent Businesses (CFIB)

The federation offers assistance and advocacy to small businesses across Canada.
cfib-fcei.ca/en

Canadian Marketing Association

The CMA originated in the 1960s and now has over 400 corporate members. It defines itself as an organization that "can help you grow your business, increase your team's marketing knowledge and safeguard your industry marketplace."
the-cma.org

Canadian's Internet Business (CIB)

Based in British Columbia, CIB describes itself as offering "tools, resources, legitimate opportunities, strategies and information from a Canadian perspective. The information provided will often be helpful to our friends in other countries who would like to do business with Canadians as well." They have a tab devoted to e-marketing, with pages that contain articles and links to dozens of valuable online resources.
canadiansinternet.com

Chief Content Officer

This is an online publication that offers a free subscription. It's geared toward content marketers and the tools they need, so go sign up!
contentmarketinginstitute.com/cco-digital/

Direct Marketing News

This is a general interest and information site that offers articles, podcasts, webcasts, and much more. It's one you'll refer back to again and again!
dmnews.com

The Interactive Advertising Bureau of Canada (IAB)

"The national voice and thought leader of the Canadian interactive marketing and advertising industry. We are the only trade association exclusively dedicated to the development and promotion of the digital marketing and advertising sector in Canada." IAB represents advertisers, ad agencies, educational organizations, and media companies, among others. The website offers a good number of resources, including podcasts, a newsletter, courses, a video library, and more.

iabcanada.com

Magazines Canada

This site is all about the Canadian magazine business, with an extensive directory of magazine addresses and websites, which is great for reaching out for advertising and marketing inquiries, as well as the possibility of stories about your business.

magazinescanada.ca

Marketing Week

Another treasure trove of information and advice, this London-based site offers insights into marketing that, while British-based, are useful no matter where in the world you are. Bookmark this site and use it often!

marketingweek.com

Newspapers Canada

From their LinkedIn profile: "The Canadian Community Newspapers Association (CCNA) and the Canadian Newspaper Association (CNA) are two separate organizations that partnered to form Newspapers Canada, creating one strong industry voice for newspapers in Canada." This is a great site for information on the Canadian newspaper industry, which will be very helpful when you're doing research for possible advertising and marketing.

nmc-mic.ca

Statistics Canada

This is a great place to start when you're looking for demographic and population data. There's a lot to explore here.

statcan.gc.ca

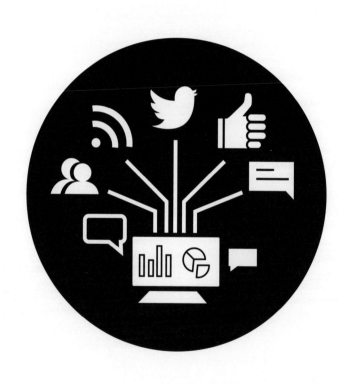

ABOUT THE AUTHOR

Tim Rayborn is a writer, educator, historian, musician, and researcher, with more than twenty years of professional experience. He is a prolific author, with a number of books and articles to his name, and more on the way. He has written on topics from the academic to the amusing to the appalling, including medieval and modern history, the arts (music, theater, and dance), food and wine, business, social studies, and works for business and government publications. He's also been a ghostwriter for various clients.

Based in the San Francisco Bay Area, Tim lived in England for seven years, studying for an M.A. and Ph.D. at the University of Leeds. He has a strong academic background but enjoys writing for general audiences.

He is also an acclaimed classical and world musician, having appeared on more than forty recordings, and he has toured and performed in the United States, Canada, Europe, North Africa, and Australia over the last twenty-five years. During that time, he has learned much about the business of arts and entertainment, and how to survive and thrive when traveling and working in intense environments.

For more, visit timrayborn.com.

INDEX

A

A/B trial, 21
ad design, tips for, 65
advertising, definition of, 15
affiliate marketing, 84–85
alcohol, consumption of at events, 108, 126
analog radio, advertising over, 60–61
analytics, for websites, 23, 31, 92, 97
audience, 7, 15, 18, 19, 22, 23, 29, 63, 66, 68, 75, 79, 82, 84, 128
automation software, 34

B

blogs, for internet marketing, 6, 24, 25, 27, 31, 33, 34, 47, 53, 82, 85, 90, 93, 98
budget, for marketing, 2, 12, 24–25, 27, 31, 59, 61, 62, 65, 67, 72, 73, 75, 76, 79, 81, 86, 94, 116, 133
builder campaigns, 27
business cards, 43, 47, 105, 106, 109, 113, 117, 122
business sponsorship, 70, 73

C

calendar listing, as type of press release, 77
calls to action, 40, 65
case studies, 34
casual networks, 45
celebrity endorsements, 13, 56–57, 117
chambers of commerce, 45, 133
charities, marketing with, 12, 49, 64, 73, 76, 104, 108, 109, 110, 128, 129
charity events, ideas for supporting, 64, 104, 108, 110, 128
co-branding, 30
college and university contacts, networking via, 48
community service group events, ideas for, 124–25
competition, 10, 20, 25, 71, 72, 117
conferences, tips for attending, 34, 70, 103, 104, 112–13, 115, 118, 121
consistency, in marketing, 30, 61
contact networks, 45
content marketing, 84, 87, 88

cultural events, ideas for, 127

customers, 6, 10, 11, 12, 13, 14, 15, 18, 21, 22, 23, 28, 29, 31, 33, 34, 37, 46, 51, 52, 54, 58, 73, 75, 76, 80, 82, 88, 91, 94, 95, 102, 107, 115, 131

D

demands, 10

design, of marketing materials, 30, 43, 65, 67, 80, 89

display ads, 87

door drops, 79

dream client, 29

driver campaigns, 27

E

elevator pitch, 105

email networking, 39

entrepreneur and small business organizations, 111

ethics, 30

exclusive website content, 34

expert endorsements, 56, 57

F

Facebook, marketing via, 33, 46, 53, 87, 96, 97, 98, 101, 131

family, networking via, 44, 48

field trials, 21

focus groups, 21, 23

follow-up, when networking, 40, 52, 53

food gatherings, ideas for, 110, 126, 127

food or wine-tasting events, 110

former coworkers, networking via, 49

fundraisers for nonprofits and charities, 73, 109, 110, 128

G

green marketing, 14

guerilla marketing, 14

H

happy hour, ideas for, 33, 126, 127

I

in-person meetings, 41, 52, 102

influencer marketing, 13

influencers, 86, 117

Instagram, marketing via, 33, 86, 96, 99, 101, 131

interviews, 21, 23, 57

investors, 27, 84, 115

K

keyword marketing, 14

L

leads, 33, 48, 109

lectures and talks, 110

LinkedIn, marketing via, 33, 46, 53, 99, 112, 131

local magazines, advertising in, 66

local newspapers, advertising in, 64

local television, advertising on, 62

logo, 30, 97

M

mailed flyers, 79

mailing lists, for internet marketing, 33, 34, 71, 76, 85, 88, 90, 115, 116, 128

marketing concept, 11–12

marketing, definition of, 15

metadata, 92

mission statements, 28

moderator, for round table events, 118, 119

N

national magazines, advertising in, 67

national newspapers, advertising in, 64–65

national television, advertising on, 62

native advertising, 87

needs, 10

networking, 32, 33, 34, 35–36, 37, 38, 39, 42, 43, 45, 47, 48, 51, 72, 88, 104, 108, 109, 121, 126, 129 networking events, 47, 104, 109, 129

newsletters, for internet marketing, 27, 33, 47, 84, 85

nonprofits, marketing with, 30, 73, 109

O

one-on-one networking, 33, 36, 102

organizer, for round table events, 119

outdoor sporting events, ideas for, 127

P

pay-per-click, 94

personal networks, 48–49

phone books, advertising in, 68–69

phone networking, 40–41

Pinterest, marketing via, 100–101, 131

podcasts, for internet marketing, 6, 87, 88

poll, 34

press release, 71, 77–78, 116, 128

primary research, 20

pro bono sponsorship, 74

product concept, 11

production concept, 11

professional associations, 46

psychographics, 23

public testimonials, 57

Q

Quality Score, 95

questionnaires, 21, 23

R

referrals, 41, 46, 48, 54, 55

regional magazines, advertising in, 66

relationship marketing, 13

reliable revenue, 24

Return on Investment (ROT), 67, 68, 74

reviews, from customers, 16, 56, 57, 91

round table events, tips for attending and participating in, 88, 118, 119, 120

S

Search Engine Marketing (SEM), 93–95

Search Engine Results Page (SERP), 92

secondary research, 20

selling concept, 11

SEO, 14, 16, 28, 33, 86, 89, 92, 93, 94

SiriusXM Radio Canada, advertising over, 61

Snapchat, marketing via, 96, 100

social media, 6, 14, 20, 23, 24, 25, 27, 28, 30, 31, 33, 34, 46, 49, 53, 55, 56, 57, 71, 75, 83, 86, 87, 88, 90, 96, 97, 100, 101, 113, 115, 116, 117, 128, 131

social media advertising, 87, 96

social proof, 14, 56, 58, 86, 90

societal marketing concept, 12

statement/message, 19

streamed radio services, advertising over, 61

success stories, 34

surveys, 21

swag bag, 117

SWOT analysis, 26

T

tag line, 30, 44

target demographics, 31, 61, 87, 100

target market, 21, 22, 23, 25, 26, 32, 70, 82, 86, 87, 94, 97, 98, 115

trade shows, tips for attending and presenting at, 34, 115, 118

V

viral marketing, 14

volunteer and community organizations, networking via, 49

volunteer work, 74, 110

W

wants, 10

webinar, for internet marketing, 88

weekly schedule, for marketing, 31

word of mouth, 14, 34, 38, 50, 51, 54, 90

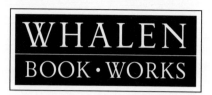

PUBLISHING PRACTICAL & CREATIVE NONFICTION

Whalen Book Works is a small, independent book publishing company based in Kennebunkport, Maine, that combines top-notch design, unique formats, and fresh content to create truly innovative gift books.

Our unconventional approach to bookmaking is a close-knit, creative, and collaborative process among authors, artists, designers, editors, and booksellers. We publish a small, carefully curated list each season, and we take the time to make each book exactly what it needs to be.

We believe in giving back. That's why we plant one tree for every ten books sold. Your purchase supports a tree in the Rocky Mountain National Park.

Get in touch!

Visit us at **WHALENBOOKS.COM**
or write to us at
68 North Street, Kennebunkport, ME 04046

TAKE YOUR CAREER
TO THE NEXT LEVEL!